Praise for *He Calls Me by the Thunder* . . .

▼ "[*He Calls Me by the Thunder*] challenges the reader to remember the hard learned lessons of spiritual oppression and spiritual growth. The book is thought provoking and insightful. It is a must for those who value healthy living."

Dr. Anthony P. Young, *Past President*
Denver-Rocky Mountain Association of
Black Psychologists

▼ "The book alternates historical facts about African-American slaves with parallels to modern-day slavery of the spirit."

Rocky Mountain News

▼ "The achievement of Mrs. Symonette's book is that it links contemporary forms of enslavement (racism, alcoholism, illiteracy, etc.) with the concrete enslavement and torture of slaves historically. Slavery is more than a metaphor in the life of Christians today, just as certainly as in the case of African Americans throughout history. This book, however, offers insight and guidance into true liberation that can spring from our hearts and empower us to sing a new slave song."

Bryan P. Stone, Ph.D.,
Associate Professor of Theology
Nazarene Bible College

▼ "Lonzie Symonette is a sensitive and serious interpreter of life, consequently her work, *He Calls Me by the Thunder*, connects history with the present struggle of Black Americans in a way only a few could capture. The book is intuitive and creative; it is a powerful lift for the soul."

Vinton R. Anderson, *President*
World Council of Churches,
Presiding Bishop, 5th Episcopal District
African Methodist Episcopal Church

HE CALLS ME BY THE THUNDER

LONZIE SYMONETTE

Publishers Since 1798

THOMAS NELSON PUBLISHERS

Nashville

Published in Nashville, Tennessee, by Thomas Nelson, Inc., Publishers, and distributed in Canada by Word Communications, Ltd., Richmond, British Columbia, and in the United Kingdom by Word (UK), Ltd., Milton Keynes, England.

Library of Congress Cataloging-in-Publication Data

Symonette, Lonzie.
  [New slave song]
  He calls me by the thunder: meditations on freedom / Lonzie Symonette.
    p.   cm.
  Originally published: A new slave song. Colorado Springs, Colo. : LMS Publishers, c1992.
  Includes bibliographical references.
  ISBN 0-7852-8174-6
  1. Freedom (Theology)—Meditations.   2. Afro-Americans—Prayer-books and devotions—English.   I. Title.
[BT810.2.S96   1993]   93-6401
242.089ʹ96073—dc20   CIP

Printed in the United States of America
2 3 4 5 6 7 - 00 99 98 97 96

DEDICATION

To my Lord, who continues to encourage me. In 2 Samuel 7:3 God said, *"Go ahead and do it, for the* LORD *is with you"* (NIV).

To some slaves long dead who knew this story would someday be told.

CONTENTS

ACKNOWLEDGMENTS

▼ Thanks to many special people who never stopped praying, giving me smiles, or words of faith during the fourteen year period of witnessing God's promise of this book fulfilled. Thanks also to my husband, Norman, who stuck by me. Thanks to Erika and Stephanie, our daughters, who were very young fourteen years ago (Erika eight years old and Stephanie five) and could not believe that Mom was writing a book. However, after seeing I was serious in my writing endeavors, they cooperated. They helped with household duties, encouraged me, and allowed me to write sometimes for at least an hour without an interruption.

PREFACE

▼ Heavy rain, flashing lightning, and roaring thunder caused our pet dog, Buster, to find a hiding place under the bed.

As the powerful thunderbolts shook our house, Mama would tell us, "Hush, God is talking." We unplugged the television, sat quietly, or went to bed until the storm ceased.

I never questioned my parents about their mysterious sayings. These were old, wise tales I figured must have been handed down from the days of slavery.

Parent and child communications have changed tremendously, and not all has changed for the best. But not so long ago when I was a child, I listened, respected and accepted what my parents said, especially when they talked about God. I have learned that many of their sayings were not just old, wise tales handed down by oral tradition. The Bible says, "God thunders marvelously with His voice; / He does great things which we cannot comprehend" (Job 37:5). And the gospel of John records, "A voice came from heaven . . . the people who stood by and heard it said that it had thundered" (12:28–29).

The spiritual "Steal Away," that was used as a signal song by my ancestors, depicts the voice of Jesus calling his people. This spiritual assured the slaves that God loathed their bondage and was majestically calling them to freedom. One verse says,

> My Lord, he calls me,
> He calls me by the thunder,
> The trumpet sounds within'a my soul,
> I ain't got long to stay here.

By the wonders of nature—his handiwork, God promised the slaves that soon he would bring divine deliverance and blessing.

For those enslaved this was no *by and by, pie in the sky, one day when I reach the kingdom* kind of promise.

> The kingdom which the poor may enter is not merely an eschatological longing for escape to a transcendent reality, nor is it an inward serenity which eases unbearable suffering. Rather, it is God encountering man in the very depths of his being-in-the-world and releasing him from all human evils . . . which hold him captive. The repentant man knows that God's ultimate kingdom is in the future, yet even now it breaks through like a ray of light upon the darkness of the oppressed.[1]

Humanity is diverse; the world is filled with many wonderful cultures. We are a multicultural world commonly bonded by the fact that historically all humans are descendants of Africa.[2] "And He has made from one blood every nation of men to dwell on all the face of the earth . . ." (Acts 17:26).

Using the tool of analogy, *He Calls Me by the Thunder* enables readers of all colors to visualize themselves as the nineteenth-century African Americans who were physically enslaved. By the voice of the Almighty, we are all called by God to experience freedom through the shed blood of Jesus, the suffering servant. Jesus is our liberator, who "[b]ecoming a slave himself, . . . opens realities of human existence formerly closed to man. Through an encounter with Jesus, man now knows the full meaning of God's action in history and man's place within it."[3] (See also Phil. 2:7 AMPLIFIED BIBLE.)

God's call to the oppressed, God's desire, is for us to sing new songs of power, victory, and praise to his name. He calls us freely to worship him.

In the Old Testament, a new song celebrated a new act of divine deliverance or blessing. A new song was a signal, a call to praise God. Moses and the Israelites sang a song to the Lord for their deliverance from Pharaoh and his mighty officers who drowned in the Red Sea (Exodus 15).

In this book I have researched historical facts and offered devotional truths to correlate physical slavery with spiritual slavery, which affects *all* humankind. *He Calls Me by the Thunder* is a record of slaves set free from the wicked master, Satan. It is a story of individuals struggling to gain the right of choice. "Do not let sin reign. . . . [S]in shall not have dominion over you" (Rom. 6:12, 14).

The voice of God is associated with a natural phenomenon that we can readily identify— thunder. The awesome power and fury of crashing thunder is a hyperbole of the sound of God's voice to his people. Psalm 29:3–4 says, "The voice of the LORD is over the waters; the God of glory thunders, the LORD thunders over the mighty waters. / The voice of the LORD is powerful" (NIV).

Hear God's voice through the reading of these pages. Listen to his call to you, because "The LORD will cause [us] to hear his majestic voice . . . with cloudburst, thunderstorm and hail" (Isa. 30:30 NIV).

INTRODUCTION

▼ My great-great-grandmother was a slave. Twenty-one years after the signing of the *Emancipation Proclamation* by Abraham Lincoln, her daughter Carey, my great-grandmother, was born free. And though slavery seems to have happened a long time ago, it was really quite recent—for that same great-grandmother was an honored guest at my wedding twenty-five years ago.

This early period of American history has been captured in music. My ancestors worked from sunup until sundown in all weather conditions. They labored from childhood until extreme old age. The songs my ancestors sang as they worked long, hot hours in the fields expressed their longing for freedom and a new life. The songs expressed the torture, the hatred, and the cruelty they endured. The songs revealed their deep faith in God. They were the heart cries of an oppressed people. This music has become an important part of our American heritage. These songs are still sung and appreciated today.

I never experienced the kind of slavery that my ancestors endured but I have struggled against another type of slavery—one common to all humanity. It is the bondage of sin.

The history of the African American is rooted in Africa, the second largest continent in the world. Millions of Africans were uprooted from their native villages and shipped to the New World.

Langston Hughes and Milton Meltzer describe the terrible passage:

> The sea lane across the Atlantic which the slave ships followed from the Gulf of Mexico or the Spanish Main was known as the "Middle Passage." Sailing vessels took many weeks to traverse the Western Ocean.
>
> During the long voyages many slaves died, for they were stacked like logwood in dank holds, chained together and allowed on deck only a few minutes per day for fresh air and exercise. In bad weather they got neither. The food was often spoiled, the water stagnant, their quarters filthy. For each five slaves delivered safely to the Americas, historians estimate that one perished on the way. Some slaves committed suicide by jumping into the water, or even by swallowing their own tongues. Those who rebelled were often shot down or beaten to death on shipboard.[1]

We are all slaves. The spiritual slavery of all humankind to sin is worse than the horrors, struggles, and perilous physical slavery of my people on the plantation. May I show you through my ancestral eyes the similarity of physical slavery to spiritual slavery? By comparing two evils, I will show many forms of bondage. The heart cries and the songs of the slaves that were created and sung on the weary road to liberation reveal a desire for freedom.

I trust you will reap the blessings of confidence, assurance, and eternal freedom that are found only in Christ Jesus.

Through combining documentation, slave narratives, slave songs, and devotionals with my personal feelings and experiences, we will celebrate freedom. Together, we will hear a new song that commemorates deliverance from bondage and gives praise to the Deliverer. Let me sing you a new slave song.

Lonzie Symonette
Colorado Springs, Colorado

CHAPTER 1

A NEW SLAVE SONG

Now these are the judgments which you shall set before them: If you buy a Hebrew servant, he shall serve six years; and in the seventh he shall go out free and pay nothing. If he comes in by himself, he shall go out by himself; if he comes in married, then his wife shall go out with him. If his master has given him a wife, and she has borne him sons or daughters, the wife and her children shall be her master's, and he shall go out by himself. But if the servant plainly says, "I love my master, my wife, and my children; I will not go out free," then his master shall bring him to the judges. He shall also bring him to the door, or to the doorpost, and his master shall pierce his ear with an awl; and he shall serve him forever.

(Ex. 21:1–6)

▼

Slave songs are part of the American heritage. Many of us have heard them, and sung them; we know the words and the melodies. Today they are sung in church services, at family gatherings, on long bus rides, and in songfests.

But they are now sung in a festive mood— without the pain.

They were created in the crucible of slavery where crusted blood formed over whip-lash cuts and lasting scars rose from branding-iron burns. The feelings and pain expressed in these songs come from those beaten with hard-knuckled fists and thick-booted kicks—those who had dirt floor shacks for living quarters, and who wept on lonely nights because loved ones had been sold to another master.

Fortunately, I was born free, so I never experienced this kind of slavery. But I have experienced the bondage to sin whose evil slavemaster is Satan. And this is a slavery even more horrid than that of my ancestors: "Slavery to Satan's control is far more tragic than slavery

2

to man, even though this is contrary to the moral law of God."[1]

I, too, have experienced an Emancipation Proclamation. The one who freed me was Christ. Because he freed me from bondage to sin and from eternal death, I am willing to become his slave of love, to do my new master's every bidding.

Deborah the prophetess sang thanks to God for victory in battle: "I, even I, will sing to the LORD" (Judg. 5:3). The psalmist said, "Sing to the LORD a new song!" (Ps. 96·1). In the tradition of my ancestors, I also sing.

Sometimes while picking greens out of my vegetable garden for dinner, taking an early morning walk, washing dishes, or enjoying the beauty of the majestic snowcapped Rocky Mountains I start singing. I have received warnings that were more like threats from my daughters, "Our friends are coming over, *please,* do not start singing." A smiling neighbor told me, "I walked by your home today, and I heard you singing."

I sing songs of joy, praise, and worship. "And he hath put a new song in my mouth, even praise unto our God" (Ps. 40:3 KJV).

I have gained a dignity which my ancestors were not allowed. I have worth, status, value, and a new, refreshing view of life.

I have a new slave song.

Consider:
Christ came to set the soul, mind, and body free from Satan's control.

Pray:
Thank you, Lord, for calling me to an abundant life. I am free from the power of sin over me.

CHAPTER 2

GOD'S BOND SLAVE

Do you not know that to whom you present yourselves slaves to obey, you are that one's slaves whom you obey, whether of sin leading to death, or of obedience leading to righteousness? But God be thanked that though you were slaves of sin, yet you obeyed from the heart that form of doctrine to which you were delivered. And having been set free from sin, you became slaves of righteousness. I speak in human terms because of the weakness of your flesh. For just as you presented your members as slaves of uncleanness, and of lawlessness leading to more lawlessness, so now present your members as slaves of righteousness for holiness. For when you were slaves of sin, you were free in regard to righteousness. What fruit did you have then in the things of which you are now ashamed? For the end of those things is death. But now having been set free from sin, and having become slaves of God, you have your fruit to holiness, and the end, everlasting life.

(Rom. 6:16–22)

▼

People do not like the idea of being servants, and they certainly reject the idea of being slaves. Even to serve someone briefly is distasteful to most people. And many of us seem so bent on serving ourselves.

God's Old Testament plan for servanthood provided for the freedom of one who had served someone for six years, as explained in Exodus 21:1–6 and Deuteronomy 15:12–18. After serving for six years, the servant was free. However, the servant could choose to continue working for his master, rather than have his freedom. In that case, the servant's ear would be pierced, and he would become a bond servant—one who was so devoted to his master that he willingly served him the rest of his life.

Romans 6 shows us that we are the slaves of whomever or whatever we obey—good influences, bad influences, or ourselves. When we do only

Published by LMS Publishers, ll261 Palmers Green Drive, Suite A, Peyton, CO. 80831-8169.

Telephone/Fax (719) 495-7348, E Mail lonziem@mindspring.com.

Unless otherwise noted, Scripture quotations are from the NEW KING JAMES VERSION of the Bible. Copyright©1979, 1980, 1982, Thomas Nelson, Inc., Publishers.

Scripture quotations noted NIV are taken from the HOLY BIBLE, NEW INTERNATIONAL VERSION®, Copyright©1973, 1978, 1984 by International Bible Society. Used by permission of Zondervan Bible Publishing House. All rights reserved.

The "NIV" and "NEW INTERNATIONAL VERSION" trademarks are registered in the United States requires the permission of International Bible Society.

Scripture quotations noted KJV are from The Holy Bible. KING JAMES VERSION.

Scripture quotations noted TLB are from The Living Bible (Wheaton, Illinois: Tyndale House Publishers, 1971) and are used by permission).

Scripture quotations noted AMPLIFIED BIBLE are from THE AMPLIFIED BIBLE: Old Testament. Copyright©1962, 1964 by Zondervan Publishing House (used by permission); and from THE AMPLIFIED NEW TESTAMENT. Copyright©1958 by the Lockman Foundation (used by permission).

Scripture quotations noted NASB are from THE NEW AMERICAN STANDARD BIBLE, Copyright©1960, 1962, 1963, 1968, 1971, 1972, 1973, 1975, 1977 by The Lockman Foundation and are used by permission.

Scripture quotation noted TEV are from the Good News Bible, Old Testament©1976 by the American Bible Society; New Testament©1966, 1971, 1976 American Bible Society. Used by permission.

Printed in the United States of America

ISBN 0-9633-078-4-3

LMS Publishers
11261 Palmers Green Drive, Suite A
Peyton, Colorado 80831-8169
Telephone/Fax   (719) 495-7348
E Mail   lonziem@mindspring.com

what we feel like doing, we are slaves of our own selfish desires!

The word *servant* means one who gives according to the will of another, one who is ardently devoted to another. A slave is absolutely subject to another and completely dominated by a master.

The Lord desires his children to be so ardently devoted to him that they become his bond slaves—bound by their love for him.

Consider:
Who are you really serving?

Pray:
Lord, I trust you completely and yield myself to you today.

CHAPTER 3

EQUIANO'S SERENDIPITY

For the love of Christ compels us, because we judge thus: that if One died for all, then all died; and He died for all, that those who live should live no longer for themselves, but for Him who died for them and rose again. Therefore, from now on, we regard no one according to the flesh. Even though we have known Christ according to the flesh, yet now we know Him thus no longer. Therefore, if anyone is in Christ, he is a new creation; old things have passed away; behold, all things have become new. Now all things are of God, who has reconciled us to Himself through Jesus Christ, and has given us the ministry of reconciliation, that is, that God was in Christ reconciling the world to Himself, not imputing their trespasses to them, and has committed to us the word of reconciliation. Now then, we are ambassadors for Christ, as though God were pleading through us: we implore you on Christ's behalf, be reconciled to God.

(2 Cor. 5:14–20)

▼

Eleven-year-old Olandah Equiano was captured from Benin, a famous black empire dating back to the 1400s. The Benin of yesterday has been incorporated into present-day Nigeria. Equiano had never seen many of the sights he was about to view on the horrid slave ship.

He narrates a serendipity experience:

During our passage I first saw flying fish which surprised me very much: they frequently flew across the ship, and many of them fell on the deck.

I also first saw the use of the quadrant. I had often with astonishment seen the mariners make observations with it, and I could not think what it meant. They took notice of my surprise: and one of them, willing to increase it, as well as to gratify my curiosity, made me one day look through it. The clouds appeared to me to be land, which disappeared as they passed along.

This heightened my wonder; and I was now more persuaded than ever that I was in another world, and that everything about me was magic.[1]

Being kidnapped by the slave traders introduced the slave to a new world, but none of it was lovely and delightful as Equiano's day on the deck of the ship.

Similarly, when I became a captive to my new master, I was introduced into a new and wonderful world. The awareness of God's love and care for me flooded my total being. This new experience of agape love helped me to respect and accept others as well as love myself. This scripture is characteristic of the new world experience, "Therefore if any man be in Christ, he is a new creature: old things are passed away; behold, all things are become new" (2 Cor. 5:17 KJV).

As Equiano, I too, before meeting Christ, was a slave to another system—the world's system. Galatians says, "So also, when we were children, we were in slavery under the basic principles of the world" (4:3 NIV). The lack of agape love shackles and destroys the power of our will to love others. The power to be able to forgive and love ourselves is crushed by the world's system.

Consider:

Observe closely whom or what you are obeying today.

Pray:

Lord, give me the willingness to surrender completely to you.

CHAPTER 4

THE WAY OUT

"Let not your heart be troubled; you believe in God, believe also in Me. In My Father's house are many mansions; if it were not so, I would have told you. I go to prepare a place for you. And if I go and prepare a place for you, I will come again and receive you to Myself; that where I am, there you may be also. And where I go you know, and the way you know."

Thomas said to Him, "Lord, we do not know where You are going, and how can we know the way?"

Jesus said to him, "I am the way, the truth, and the life. No one comes to the Father except through Me."

(John 14:1–6)

▼

James Weldon Johnson (1871–1938) was the first black man admitted to the Florida bar. In 1930 he became a professor of creative literature at Fisk University, and from 1934 until his death held the title of visiting professor at New York University. He wrote scores of poems, one of which was entitled "O Black and Unknown Bard," a portion of which follows:

Heart of what slave poured out such melody
As 'Steal Away to Jesus'?
On its strains His spirit must have nightly
    floated free, though still about his hands he felt
    his chains.

... O black slave singers, gone, forgot, unfamed,
    You—you alone, of all the long, long line
Of those who've sung untaught, unknown,
    unnamed,
You sang a race from wood and stone to Christ.[1]

The slave's singing was sometimes the only way to express inner thoughts, buried hopes, and broken hearts. To sing from the heart gave the slave, as it gives me, an avenue of escape.

In today's world, slavery wears disguises. Executives wearing the latest fashions in business attire who think they are climbing the corporate ladder to riches and prestige instead find themselves shackled to a ball and chain called success. "I must reach my quota. I must make more money, move to a better neighborhood, drive an expensive car, have the right household pet, and be a member of the right social club. I must attend an acceptable church, without appearing too religious. The children must attend the right school and of course, attend the most prestigious college, and obtain an influential summer job."

The wife and mother must keep a model home and prepare food the way we see it in women's magazines. She must keep a slim, trim figure, even if her body frame is designed to carry more than 125 pounds. She is enslaved by the need to have the most gifted and talented children.

Young people are enslaved to peer pressure. They must wear the most fashionable, designer clothes. They believe that personal acceptance is based on being a member of the right social group. Young people are pressured to use the latest slang and walk the latest walk. They must have the right haircut and experiment with drugs, alcohol, and premarital sex.

The twentieth-century person may say, "I am sure glad slavery is abolished. I am glad that there are no more slave ships. No more cramped, dark holds packed with men, women, and children. Slavery is all over."

This is not true.

Slavery still exists in different forms. The evil slave master, Satan, is also known as the "angel of light." He disguises slavery.

We do not have to be shackled to anything. There is a way out, a way to freedom. Jesus said, "I am the way" (John 14:6). We can steal away to Jesus as James Weldon Johnson described in his poem when he said the slaves "sang a race from wood and stone to Christ."

Christ removes the camouflage of spiritual slavery and gives us life in all its fullness.

Consider:

Make a list of all known hindrances in your life that prevent complete obedience to Christ.

Pray:

Father, in the name of Jesus, break the iron chains that hinder me from becoming all that you have designed for me. Holy Spirit, fill me, control me, and make me whole. Thank you, Lord, for freedom.

CHAPTER 5

LIBERTY IN THE TRUTH

Then Jesus said to those Jews who believed Him, "If you abide in My word, you are My disciples indeed. And you shall know the truth, and the truth shall make you free."

They answered Him, "We are Abraham's descendants, and have never been in bondage to anyone. How can you say, 'You will be made free'?"

Jesus answered them, "Most assuredly, I say to you, whoever commits sin is a slave of sin. And a slave does not abide in the house forever, but a son abides forever. Therefore if the Son makes you free, you shall be free indeed."

(John 8:31–36)

Pilate therefore said to Him, "Are You a king then?" Jesus answered, "You say rightly that I am a king. For this cause I was born, and for this cause I have come into the world, that I should bear witness to the truth. Everyone who is of the truth hears My voice."

Pilate said to Him, "What is truth?" And when he had said this, he went out again to the Jews, and said to them, "I find no fault in Him at all."

(John 18:37–38)

▼

Pilate resisted the possibility of singing a new song when he rejected Christ's answer to his question, "What is truth?"

Jesus had answered that question even before Pilate asked it. John 18:37 tells us "You say correctly that I am a king. For this I have been born, and for this I have come into the world, to bear witness to the truth. Everyone who is of the truth hears My voice" (NASB). Everything Jesus taught was true.

Only truth can give us the freedom that we need and want. We cannot have total freedom until we know Christ.

We may want to be free of a habit, a physical deficiency, a wrong attitude, or unpleasant circumstances. We may want someone to come into our lives and help us. Jesus will do that if we ask him. He is waiting for us to give him permission.

The truth of the gospel sets us free. When Jesus told the Pharisees that the truth would make them free, they declared that they were not slaves and did not need freedom. Jesus answered them, "Everyone who commits sin is the slave of sin. . . . If therefore the Son shall make you free, you shall be free indeed" (John 8:34, 36 NASB).

Consider:
It is good to listen to the liberating voice of Jesus in his Word.

Pray:
Lord, I want to sing a new song based on your truth.

CHAPTER 6

ESCAPE

Stretch out Your hand from above;
Rescue me and deliver me out of great waters,
From the hand of foreigners,
Whose mouth speaks lying words,
And whose right hand is a right hand of
 falsehood.
I will sing a new song to You, O God;
On a harp of ten strings I will sing praises to You,
The One who gives salvation to kings,
Who delivers David His servant
From the deadly sword.
Rescue me and deliver me from the hand of
 foreigners,

Whose mouth speaks lying words,
And whose right hand is a right hand of
 falsehood.

(Ps. 144:7–11)

▼

John Lovell, Jr., in *Black Song: The Forge and the Flame*, said, "if you have true twenty-four-hour-a-day, seven-day-a-week religious faith, you insist upon exploding or exuding it into song every time you can."[1]

I never sang before I became a Christian. I could not carry a tune in an empty bucket, which was reflected by the grade of "D" that I earned in choir. The facts are that I frustrated the poor choir director so much that he made me stand in the classroom closet and sometimes kept me after school for messing up the whole alto section.

Now I sing all the time—with joy, and sometimes even on key!

Many things affect our lives but music can have a profound effect on us. If we are depressed or discouraged, the sounds of joyful music can work wonders. God becomes a master musician and gives us music that soothes and calms us or gives us the pep we need. The scriptures refer to it often. God gives us a new song.

My ancestors used song as I do today. As a twentieth-century African American, I use songs of praise and worship as an escape from the stress and expectations of the world. The roles of wife, homemaker, and mother of two daughters have demands that can be overwhelming without the strong support of Christ, my anchor and my solid rock. The pressure release valve of song is a constant part of my life.

Englishman William Faux kept a journal of his visit to America (1818–1820) and published it in 1823 under the title of *Memorable Days in America*. Faux described the singing of the galley slaves: "regulated by the motion of their oars: this music . . . was barbarously harmonious. The text of their songs abounded in praise or satire, depending on whether their masters were kind or unkind. The following year Faux had a chance to hear singing in a black church where the minister, like the congregation, was black. This singing was merry, like the African singing."[2]

Today I sing with great joy. With Christ in my life, I cannot help but burst out in a song or at least hum sometimes.

Great men of the Bible said, "Hear, O kings; give ear, O rulers! / I—to the LORD, I will sing, / I will sing praise to the LORD, the God of Israel" (Judg. 5:3 NASB). King David said, "I will sing a new song" (Ps. 144:9 NIV).

I join my voice with the voices of many. I, too, will sing a new song.

Consider:

What is your favorite hymn? Sing it while in the car, walking, or taking a shower.

Pray:

Lord, I know that you hear my heart singing praises even if the tone is off-key.

CHAPTER 7

SECURITY

For as many as are led by the Spirit of God, these are sons of God. For you did not receive the spirit of bondage again to fear, but you received the Spirit of adoption by whom we cry out, "Abba, Father." The Spirit Himself bears witness with our spirit that we are children of God, and if children, then heirs—heirs of God and joint heirs with Christ, if indeed we suffer with Him, that we may also be glorified together.

For I consider that the sufferings of this present time are not worthy to be compared with the glory which shall be revealed in us. For the earnest expectation of the creation eagerly waits for the revealing of the sons of God.

(Rom. 8:14–19)

▼

Clarence White was a concert violinist, a composer of black music, a historian, respected critic, and teacher. His research revealed the spiritual, "'Nobody Knows the Trouble I've Seen' sprang from the heart of a Negro slave whose trials were almost more than he could bear. After wife and children had been sold away, he withdrew to his cabin and poured out his sorrow in this song. The mere creation or singing of such a song, from the standpoint of personal character, is a great victory over adversity."[1]

Frederick Douglass characterized spirituals by noting that "They were ones, loud, long, and deep, breathing the prayer and complaint of souls boiling over with the bitterest anguish. Every tone was a testimony against slavery, and a prayer to God for deliverance from chains."[2]

It was not unusual for slave masters to sell family members separately, often sending them far away from each other. And slave masters chose to perpetuate the lie that slaves were indifferent to these family breakups. But Africans have an unusually strong sense of family identification, and these separations were almost unbearable for the African slave. Even dead family members and ancestors "enhanced rather than forfeited their status"[3] within the family. So many spirituals and slave songs deal lyrically with this pain of separation.

The slave family was broken, stolen from its country, and torn from its culture. Slaves had to learn a new language when they were brought to America. They also learned all the other African tribal languages of the quarter community. In fact, the slaveowners deliberately separated those who spoke the same language. They were snatched away from any familiarity. Cultural roots were severed. Childhood homes and hunting grounds were left behind. Slaves were crushed, broken, and beaten. Their poignant hope for reunion was described in this consolation spiritual:

> When we all meet in heaven
> There is no parting there;
> When we all meet in heaven,
> There is parting no more.

"Certainly it is clear that the words of such songs were not nearly so important to the singer as the heartlessness and poignancy of the events which inspired them." Recognition of a similar reaction to such an experience is recorded in

Edith Talbot's *True Religion in Negro Hymns* (1922),

> Solo: 'Mother is massa gwine to sell us
>   tomorrow?
> Answer: 'Yes, yes, Yes! . . . Gwine to sell
>   us down . . .'[4]

In the family of God there is a bond that transcends color, class, and culture. Trusting faith in the Son of God bridges and builds family ties with other believers in Christ. Sometimes this spiritual bond can be stronger with strangers than with blood relatives. "[Y]ou are a member of God's very own family, citizens of God's country, and you belong in God's household with every other Christian" (Eph. 2:19b TLB).

With Christ as our master, we have rest and security. His hands hold us in a powerful bond of love. His gentle grip gives us safety. He said, "no one is able to snatch them out of My hand" (John 10:28 AMPLIFIED BIBLE).

Consider:
Are there some stolen, broken family relationships that need restoration? Contact a distant loved one. Consider if this person might even be in your own household.

Pray:

Father, I have loved ones who are outside of your household. I want them to come home to you.

CHAPTER 8

SONGS WITH AND WITHOUT WORDS

For we were saved in this hope, but hope that is seen is not hope; for why does one still hope for what he sees? But if we hope for what we do not see, we eagerly wait for it with perseverance.

Likewise the Spirit also helps in our weaknesses. For we do not know what we should pray for as we ought, but the Spirit Himself makes intercession for us with groanings which cannot be uttered. Now He who searches the hearts knows what the mind of the Spirit is, because He makes intercession for the saints according to the will of God.

And we know that all things work together for good to those who love God, to those who are the called according to His purpose.

(Rom. 8:24–28)

▼

Howard Hanson, former head of the Eastman School of Music and the 1944 winner of the Pulitzer Prize, stated: "The musical progress of a people must be judged not by [their] orchestra or by [their] opera houses, but by the music which arises spontaneously from the creative spirit existing among that people."[1]

I knew a ninety-three-year-old gentleman named Mr. Horace. He always sang his favorite songs to us when we visited him at the nursing home. He sang with a crystal-clear tone and gusto, "Do Lord, Do Lord, Do Remember Me," and "Were You There?"

Through his singing, I could feel my strong heritage. The words depicted a heartfelt, personal relationship with the Lord Jesus. Because Mr. Horace sang in a dialect I had never heard before, I listened intently. I wanted to learn the words and the beat so that my children would know the songs of their people. I later had the privilege of singing these songs at Mr. Horace's "homegoing" funeral.

As I write this section, from deep within me, an unnamed song stirs. A moan and hum combine into something that I was not taught. A hopeful, spontaneous, and meaningful melody bursts forth from my heart. This wordless song brings comfort, hope, and a depth of understanding. Others, who have heard and felt a slave song, will understand. My love for Jesus is expressed in song.

The slaves sang with purpose. John Lovell, Jr. said, "Primitive man sings . . . only when he has something definite to express. In this spontaneous expression, song and speech are often intermingled."[2] My purpose of expression is in the truth that the Lord God knows all things, even the thoughts of my heart that flow through my song.

Does music rise spontaneously from your heart? Jesus gives those who have received him enough joy to fill their lives. We can even have joy in our trials when we remember what James tells us, "My brethren, count it all joy when you fall into various trials, knowing that the testing of your faith produces patience. But let patience have its perfect work, that you may be perfect and complete, lacking nothing" (1:2–4).

God understands our wordless songs. He understands our unspeakable heartbreaks and disappointments. He knows that the hum or groan is a prayer. Sometimes a cry for help is a song without words. "[T]he Spirit himself intercedes for us with groans that words cannot express" (Rom. 8:26 NIV).

Consider:
The birds sing without words. We can too. Hum, create your own melody as a prayer to the Lord.

Pray:
Thank you, Holy Spirit, for interpreting my song.

CHAPTER 9

AUCTION BLOCK

Knowing that you were not redeemed with corruptible things, like silver or gold, from your aimless conduct received by tradition from your fathers, but with the precious blood of Christ, as of a lamb without blemish and without spot. He indeed was foreordained before the foundation of the world, but was manifest in these last times for you who through Him believe in God, who raised Him from the dead and gave Him glory, so that your faith and hope are in God.

Since you have purified your souls in obeying the truth through the Spirit in sincere love of the brethren, love one another fervently with a pure heart, having been born again, not of corruptible seed but incorruptible, through the word of God which lives and abides forever, because

"All flesh is as grass,
And all the glory of man as the flower of the
    grass.
The grass withers,
And its flower falls away,
But the word of the LORD endures forever."

Now this is the word which by the gospel was preached to you.

(1 Peter 1:18–25)

Beware lest anyone cheat you through philosophy and empty deceit, according to the tradition of men, according to the basic principles of the world, and not according to Christ.

(Col. 2:8)

▼

"Extra! Extra! New shipment of slaves." Imagine hearing these words booming through the market square, signaling the arrival of a slave ship.

Prospective buyers gathered around the auction block ready to inspect the merchandise as they would cattle. Female slaves were shamelessly prodded, touched, and fondled like produce for sale.

These exhibitions humiliated and grieved the slaves and incited deep hatred toward the slave masters.

> All these sensitivities the slave sang . . . because his song was his sole means of expressing his emotions and feelings. From these songs came the truest judgment of his character and disposition. He sang in the fields, in his cabins, in his secret meetings, in quietude to himself. He did not merely sing his sorrows and his joys. He sang his suppressed hopes and his broken, bleeding heart. He sang his rash resolutions. As his African ancestors had been doing for centuries, he lived to the hilt the cruel life handed him and sang the totality of that life.[1]

One day the redeemed of God will stand on another kind of platform before a loving, kind master, not to be manhandled, inspected, rejected, or purchased. We will stand and sing a new slave song. "They sung as it were a new song before the throne" (Rev. 14:3 KJV).

My ancestors sang the song, "No More Auction Block for Me." Our songs of praise please the Lord. Just think, no more auction blocks for us! Satan's rule is broken!

Imagine with me hearing another announcer crying out, "Extra! Extra! Spread the good news! Man is not lost forever! God has not given up on us! He has bought us out of slavery to sin by the payment of Christ's death on the cross. Satan's rule can be broken and we can reign with Christ. We can be restored to the security and significance for which we have been created—not simply in eternity, but here and now as well."[2]

Our worth and esteem are based on the love Christ displayed for us when he shed his precious blood on Calvary. The finished work of Christ crushed the destructive power of that low self-esteem and low self-worth. Cultivating a healthy self-image is a part of the transforming work of our new master—Christ.

Many people suffer from the slavery of perfectionism or self-criticism. Robert S. McGee in his book *Search for Significance* states, "Satan has deceived us. He has led us blindly down a path of destruction, captives of our inability to meet our standard consistently, and slaves of low self-esteem. Satan has shackled us in chains that keep us from experiencing the love, freedom, and purposes of Christ."[3]

Consider:

Read Revelation 14:3 and Psalm 144:9 in different translations of the Bible. Meditate on the truths of these Scriptures.

Pray:

Thank you, Jesus, for purchasing me. I delight in the fact that there will be no more auction block for me.

CHAPTER 10

HE BORE OUR SINS

Pilate answered and said to them again, "What then do you want me to do with Him whom you call the King of the Jews?"

So they cried out again, "Crucify Him!"

Then Pilate said to them, "Why, what evil has He done?" But they cried out all the more, "Crucify Him!"

So Pilate, wanting to gratify the crowd, released Barabbas to them; and he delivered Jesus, after he had scourged Him, to be crucified.

Then the soldiers led Him away into the hall called Praetorium, and they called together the whole garrison. And they clothed Him with purple; and they twisted a crown of thorns, put it on His head, and began to salute Him, "Hail, King of the Jews!" Then they struck Him on the head with a reed and spat on Him; and bowing the knee, they worshiped Him. And when they had mocked Him, they took the purple off Him, put His own clothes on Him, and led Him out to crucify Him.

(Mark 15:12–20)

▼

Historical research reveals that the raw, deliberate brutality meted out to the slave directly influenced slave songs. The master or one of his overseers would administer floggings, while other slaves were required to observe these brutal beatings.

Helen T. Catterall reported a case in June 1857, of a thirteen-year-old runaway girl who was beaten to death by an overseer using a three-ply leather strap. The courts indicted the overseer for murder and convicted him of involuntary manslaughter. The courts then recommended mercy.

The testimony of eyewitnesses to these brutalities, and advertisements from newspapers seeking the return of runaways verify the awful life of the slave. Some advertisements reported runaway slaves that had scars from whippings about the neck, cheeks, lips, chin, back, arms, thighs, and hips.

In biblical times the number of lashes was restricted. "Forty stripes he may give him, and not exceed" (Deut. 25:3 KJV).

Supposedly, thirty-nine lashes was normal punishment for a runaway slave; however, on many occasions floggings far exceeded that number. The average lash was seven to eight feet long and made of cowhide or something to cut human flesh. A whipping might be as high as seventy to one hundred lashes.[1]

Whipping was also a common punishment among the Jews. According to Roman practice, a person "was stripped, stretched with cords or thongs on a frame and beaten with cords . . . the scourge consisted of a handle with three lashes fastened to them."[2]

Pilate "had Jesus flogged. . . . They put a purple robe on him, then twisted together a crown of thorns and set it on him. . . . Again and again they struck him on the head with a staff and spit on him. . . . Then they led him out to crucify him" (Mark 15:15, 17, 19, 20 NIV).

My new master, Christ, was beaten for my sins . . . for our sins. The details of the suffering of Jesus were foretold in Isaiah 53: "But he was pierced for our transgressions, he was crushed for our iniquities; the punishment that brought us peace was upon him, and by his wounds we are healed. . . . and the LORD has laid on him the iniquity of us all" (Isa. 53:5–6 NIV).

Jesus was without sin. But because he loved us, he endured the brutality of flogging and suffered the ultimate punishment of death. His "work is essentially one of liberation. Becoming a slave himself, he opens realities of human existence formerly closed to man." Through an encounter with the cross, "through an encounter with Jesus, [we] now know the full meaning of God's action in history and [our] place within it."[3]

Consider:
Read all of Isaiah 53. Memorize verses 5 and 6.

Pray:
Lord, never let me forget how much you suffered for my salvation.

CHAPTER 11

YOU
ARE
SOMEBODY

Thus says God the LORD,
Who created the heavens and stretched them out,
Who spread forth the earth and that which
   comes from it,
Who gives breath to the people on it,
And spirit to those who walk on it:
"I, the LORD, have called You in righteousness,
And will hold Your hand;
I will keep You and give You as a covenant to the
   people,
As a light to the Gentiles,
To open blind eyes,
To bring out prisoners from the prison,

Those who sit in darkness from the prison house.
I am the LORD, that is My name;
And My glory I will not give to another,
Nor My praise to carved images.
Behold, the former things have come to pass,
And new things I declare;
Before they spring forth I tell you of them."
Sing to the LORD a new song,
And His praise from the ends of the earth,
You who go down to the sea, and all that is in it,
You coastlands and you inhabitants of them!

(Isa. 42:5–10)

▼

In my home I was taught that I was as good as—if not better than—those who would suppress me.

My ancestors did not receive this same message. Interviewed about his life as a slave, Charlie Moses remembered: "Slavery days was bitter an' I can't forgit the sufferin'. . . . God Almighty never meant for human beings to be animals. . . . We ain't like a dog or a horse."[1]

But how could the slaves prove they were people—that they were human beings just like those who beat them? The slaves battled against irrationality: "The first thing, then, which seems necessary in order to remove those prejudices which are so unjustly entertained against us is to prove that we are men—a truth which is difficult of proof only because it is difficult to imagine by what argument it can be combatted."[2]

Remember that many of the three million slaves who came from Africa were from the middle and upper classes. Many of them were artisans, skilled workers, and craftsmen.

Many were leaders. A narrative by Zamba, an African king, is written proof even of kings and queens having been kidnapped from their country. "One day in the Spring of 1839 a handsome young African whose name was Cinque was seized and carried off to be sold into slavery. The son of a Mendi Chief, he soon found himself with many others chained in a sitting position in the hold of a Portuguese vessel bound for Cuba."[3]

It is very likely that many African Americans are descendants of kings and queens. People may try to make us feel inferior. However, "The Lord God who created the heavens and . . . the earth and everything in it, and gives life and breath and spirit to everyone in all the world" (Isa. 42:5 TLB) loves and cares for all his creation.

I saw a poster that said, "God don't make junk." God does not make mistakes, and he never makes junk. All people are special to him. God is loving and gracious.

As a descendant of slaves, my childhood training, whether at home or school, included the rehearsal of the fact that "I am somebody."

You are somebody too. There is no other human being on earth exactly like you. You are custom-made. You are a special somebody to God.

He loves you and wants you to put your trust in Jesus Christ as your Savior and Lord. By his Spirit living in you, God begins the work of transforming your life so you will become more and more like Jesus. You can feel good about who you are becoming in Christ. As a servant of the Lord you can sing a new song—a song of praise.

Consider:
God made you uniquely his. Praise him!

Pray:
Thank you, Lord, for making me special. I am somebody because you love me. I will sing a new song and praise you to the end of my days.

CHAPTER 12

BRANDED

For in Christ Jesus neither circumcision nor uncircumcision avails anything, but a new creation.

And as many as walk according to this rule, peace and mercy be upon them, and upon the Israel of God.

From now on let no one trouble me, for I bear in my body the marks of the Lord Jesus.

Brethren, the grace of our Lord Jesus Christ be with your spirit. Amen.

(Gal. 6:15-18)

Slaves were branded with red-hot irons. Masters burned their own initials into the slaves' flesh. The following newspaper advertisements describe the branding marks found on the bodies of runaway slaves:

- A girl named Mary with an eye scar, many teeth missing, and the letter A branded on her cheek and forehead.
- Runaway Bill with a dogbite on his leg, scar over his eye, burn on his buttock from a piece of hot iron in the shape of a T.[1]
- A man, for going to visit his brethren without the permission of his master . . . may be caught on his way, dragged to a post, the branding-iron heated, and the name of his master or the letter branded into his cheek or on his forehead.
- For riding or going abroad in the night, or riding horses in the daytime, without leave, a slave may be whipped . . . or branded in the cheek with the letter R.[2]

While in service to the Lord, Christians receive scars from the evil slavemaster. The branding iron of self-centered living, greed, and bitterness leaves ugly marks on human hearts.

William Barclay in his commentary on Galatians tells how the apostle Paul was a slave for Christ. "Paul bore on his body the marks of his campaigns, the marks of his sufferings, the brand of the slavery of Christ. The very fact that he was marked as he was was the final proof that his one aim was to serve Christ and not to please men."[3]

Christians, who sing the "new slave song" are branded; we have marks and scars. We earn our scars as we stand against the evil spiritual battles that confront us: "I bear," said Paul, "on my body the marks of Jesus" (Gal. 6:17 NIV). As Barclay paraphrases Paul, "'My marks are scars I carry with me to be my witness to Him who will now be my rewarder.'"[4]

Consider:
What brand marks do you bear for the Lord Jesus? What scars witness to your love for God?

Pray:
Lord, it is a privilege to be branded because of my love for you.

CHAPTER 13

THE SINGING GRAPEVINE

And Jesus came and spoke to them, saying, "All authority has been given to Me in heaven and on earth. Go therefore and make disciples of all the nations, baptizing them in the name of the Father and of the Son and of the Holy Spirit, teaching them to observe all things that I have commanded you; and lo, I am with you always, even to the end of the age." Amen.

(Matt. 28:18–20)

The slaves had few means of keeping abreast of the current news. The majority could not read or write English. They often communicated through song: "One of the more constant tools that the slaves used to resist the spiritual brutality of slavery was music. In Africa music is not an art form as much as it is a means of communication."[1]

Through song or secret message, news traveled fast by a grapevine system. John Adams wrote in 1775: "The Negroes have a wonderful art of communicating intelligence among themselves, it will run several hundred miles in a week."[2]

Because songs were such a powerful and unifying tool among the slaves, "The Afro-American spiritual was perpetually threatened by the rules of the plantation . . ."[3]

The singing grapevine of the slave community would cause the telecommunication systems of today to stop and take notice.

Communication through the artful use of gestures, words, and songs enabled the slave to secretly educate and transmit thoughts and special messages. The banjo, jaw-bones, fiddle, guills, sticks, and tin pans were instruments commonly played to accompany songs.

Most of the songs, including spirituals, were important for entertaining and transmitting the values, attitudes, and sentiments of the slave community that built individual personalities and bonded the fellow slave's consciousness.

Nat Turner called his conspirators to him by singing the song "Steal Away." "The Chariot's A'coming" called out to the slave row conductor for the Underground Railroad. "Good News, Member" rejoiced and reported to all that a runaway slave had reached freedom. "Foller the Drinkin' Gourd" (the drinking gourd was the Big Dipper in the sky) mapped out part of the path followed by the Underground Railroad.[4]

The words to "Follow the Drinkin' Gourd" read like a word map. Said to have been taught to slaves by an abolitionist sailor named Peg Leg Joe, the song gives directions for running away in the spring and "using as a guide both the North-pointing Dipper and the peg-toes signs Joe would mark on dead trees along the river bank—leading to the headwaters of the Tombigbee River, and across the divide to the Ohio River and freedom."[5]

When the sun come back and first quail calls,
Follow the drinkin'-gourd,
The old man is a-waitin' to carry you to freedom,
Follow the drinkin'-gourd.

Now the river bank will make a might good road.
The dead trees will show you the way,
Left foot, peg foot, travelin' on,
Just you follow the drinkin'-gourd.

Where the little river meets the great big one,
The old man is a-waitin' to carry you to freedom,
Follow the drinkin'-gourd.

The river ends between two hills,
Follow the drinkin'-gourd.
There's another river on the other side,
Follow the drinkin'-gourd.[6]

Many biblical figures appear in slave songs: "Methuselah, de Oldest Man"; "Father Abraham"; "Wrestling Jacob and His Ladder"; "Ezekiel and His Wheel"; "David and His Harp"; "John de Holy Baptist"; "Fisherman Peter"; "Nicodemus, the Man Among the Pharisees"; "Lazarus"; and "Weeping Mary," to name a few. Few slaves could read and fewer still had access to a Bible. The biblical knowledge the slaves learned came from religious songs.

The medium of storytelling and songs taught slaves about Africa, "the nature of slavery in other slave states, the existence of the North and Canada, or the history of their home plantation, the happenings on neighboring plantations, and of the deeds and daring of Black heroes and folkheroes. Often it was through stories . . . and songs . . . that slave children learned bits of their family history."[7]

To escape the wiles of the evil one, we do not need the stars to map out our freedom as in the signal song "Follow the Drinkin' Gourd." Unafraid, we can communicate freely in prayer. Through music and singing, we can openly praise God for our freedom and the power to overcome the evil one.

The psalmist said, "The Lord is good and glad to teach the proper path to all who go astray; he will teach the ways that are right and best to those who humbly turn to him. And when we obey him, every path he guides us on is fragrant with his lovingkindness and his truth" (Ps. 25:8–10 TLB).

The twelve disciples of the Lord Jesus spread the liberating message of God's love for the world. God uses people to spread the gospel. Jesus said, ". . . you shall be My witnesses both in Jerusalem and in all Judea and Samaria, and even to the remotest part of the earth" (Acts 1:8 NASB).

Consider:

Actions speak loudly. Actively share with someone the love of Jesus.

Pray:

Lord, help me be as effective in evangelism as the slaves were in communicating.

CHAPTER 14

PIED PIPER

Oh, sing to the LORD a new song!
Sing to the LORD, all the earth.
Sing to the LORD, bless His name;
Proclaim the good news of His salvation from
   day to day.
Declare His glory among the nations,
His wonders among all peoples.

For the LORD is great and greatly to be praised;
He is to be feared above all gods.
For all the gods of the peoples are idols,
But the LORD made the heavens.
Honor and majesty are before Him;

Strength and beauty are in His sanctuary.

(Ps. 96:1–6)

▼

According to an old legend, the Pied Piper lured rats and children by playing his magic pipe.

Harriet Tubman, the Black Moses of the underground railroad who was known as General Tubman, served as a spy, nurse, scout, and cook during the Civil War. She used song to lead slaves to freedom. She ". . . acquired her general's stars from John Brown. Five feet tall, carrying to her grave bruises and ailments caused by her slave experiences, she ran away repeatedly from slave territory and carried between two and three hundred slaves with her."[1]

Tubman said she "grew up like a neglected weed, ignorant of liberty, having no experience of it." Since two of her sisters had been taken away to the chain gang, she feared being taken away every time she saw a white man. She said, "Now I've been free I know what a dreadful condition slavery is. I have seen hundreds of escaped slaves, but I never saw one who was willing to go back and be a slave. I think slavery is the next thing to hell."[2]

In spite of redoubled patrols, in spite of increasing rewards which began at $1,000 and finally reached as high as $40,000, General Harriet kept returning to slave territory, kept bringing out slaves like some omniscient, unselfish, incomparably fearless and brave Pied Piper, kept marching them along to the tunes of "Old Chariot," "Go Down, Moses," "Steal Away," "The Gospel Train Is Coming," "There's No Rain to Wet You," and "Didn't My Lord Deliver Daniel?"

General Tubman used the song "Go Down Moses" to call up candidates for transportation to free land; she also used the song "Wade in the Water" to warn her friends how to throw bloodhounds off the scent.

Have you ever thought about being a modern-day pied piper? What gift has God given you to use to help people be free from their burden of sin? Remember the saying, "You catch more flies with honey than with vinegar." Your invitation will be more alluring if it reflects the joy of a singing heart.

Consider:

Be a pied piper. Invite someone to an inspirational concert, a church social, a Sunday school class, or a Bible study.

Pray:

Lord, make me a brave pied piper of the gospel.
I want to lead others from slavery to freedom.

CHAPTER 15

THE LORD GIVES WISDOM

So that you incline your ear to wisdom,
And apply your heart to understanding;
Yes, if you cry out for discernment,
And lift up your voice for understanding,
If you seek her as silver,
And search for her as for hidden treasures;
Then you will understand the fear of the LORD,
And find the knowledge of God.
For the LORD gives wisdom;
From His mouth come knowledge and
    understanding;
He stores up sound wisdom for the upright;

He is a shield to those who walk uprightly;
He guards the paths of justice,
And preserves the way of His saints.
Then you will understand righteousness and
justice,
Equity and every good path.

(Prov. 2:2–9)

▼

Autobiographies of runaway slaves reveal "the thing which drove them to risk their lives, repeatedly, to be free, even more than cruel and unjust treatment, was the prospect of living forever in mental and spiritual darkness. There are dozens of songs on the subjects of reading and writing: "My Lord's Writing All the Time," "My Mother Got a Letter," "O' Lord, Write My Name," "Gwine to Write Massa Jesus," "De Book of Revelation God to Us Revealed," that prove this deep concern of the slave."[1]

Frederick Douglass said, "This is American slavery; no marriage—no education—the light of the gospel shut out from the dark mind of the bondmen—and he forbidden by the law to learn to read. If a mother teach her children to read ... she may be hanged by the neck. If the father attempt to give his son a knowledge of letters, he may be punished by the whip in one instance, and in another be killed, at the discretion of the court. Three million people shut out from the light of knowledge!"[2]

When Frederick Douglass was ten years old, he served in temporary service with his master's daughter. The wife of the master was teaching Douglass to read when her husband angrily stopped the lessons. Douglass' burning desire to read caused him to study carefully and to learn reading skills from white children.

He copied letters and words on walls with chalk. Somehow, he acquired his only book, *The Columbian Orator*. Possibly, the master's wife secretly gave the book to young Douglass. He read the speeches of Pitt, Fox, and Burke, with their stirring words about liberty and freedom. As a teenager, Douglass taught spelling as well as scriptures in a small country Sunday school. Douglass continued educating people at the school until slavers violently stopped him, warning him not to become another Nat Turner.

Though it was illegal for the slave to read, Jesus enjoined his servants to "search the Scriptures" (John 5:39a). Over and over the Bible says that we are to seek knowledge, wisdom, and understanding. Those who studied the Bible daily in Berea were praised in Acts 17:11.

Even today the evil slave master, Satan, would like to keep everyone ignorant of the rich promises found in God's Word. Satan has been successful in keeping thousands of people in ignorance of God's life principles. "My people are destroyed for lack of knowledge" (Hos. 4:6 KJV). To reverse the downward trend in our country, Christians should get actively involved in helping people learn God's Word. Without spiritual knowledge we are in danger of being destroyed.

Consider:
Be a godly example; faithfully teach, live, and obey God's principles in your family.

Pray:
Lord, may I never take for granted the freedom I have to study and learn about you through your Word.

CHAPTER 16

NO MORE PARTING

Who shall separate us from the love of Christ? Shall tribulation, or distress, or persecution, or famine, or nakedness, or peril, or sword? As it is written:

"For Your sake we are killed all day long;

We are accounted as sheep for the slaughter."

Yet in all these things we are more than conquerors through Him who loved us. For I am persuaded that neither death nor life, nor angels nor principalities nor powers, nor things present nor things to come, nor height nor depth, nor any other created thing, shall be able to separate us from the love of God which is in Christ Jesus our Lord.

(Rom. 8:35–39)

▼

Can you believe there was ever a society on earth where men and women could not marry? There was. Right here in America.

Many times a loving man and woman would hold hands and jump over a broom that lay on the ground to signify publicly that they were a committed couple. The rest of the slave community served as witnesses of this simple but sacred ceremony that bound together a man and woman in lieu of the traditional marriage ceremony.

After escaping from slavery in 1838, Frederick Douglass began a long career as a leading abolitionist writer. He lectured in Europe as well as in the United States on the horrors of slavery. Douglass described to an audience in Finsbury Chapel at Moorsfield on May 12, 1846, the plight of one slave couple.

A slave woman and a slave man had united themselves as man and wife in the absence of any law to protect them as man and wife. They had lived together by the permission, not by right, of their master, and they had reared a family. The master found it expedient, and for his interest, to sell them. He did not ask them their wishes in regard to the matter at all; they were not consulted. The man and woman were brought to the auctioneer's block, under the sound of the hammer. The cry was raised, "Here goes; who bids cash?"

Think of it—a man and wife to be sold! The woman was placed on the auctioneer's block; her limbs, as is customary, were brutally exposed to the purchasers, who examined her with all the freedom with which they would examine a horse. There stood the husband, powerless; no right to his wife; the master's right preeminent. She was sold.

He was next brought to the auctioneer's block. His eyes followed his wife in the distance; and he looked beseechingly, imploringly, to the man that had bought his wife to buy him also. But he was at length bid off to another person. He was about to be separated forever from her whom he loved. No word of his, nor work of his, could save him from this separation. He asked permission of his new master to go and take the hand of his wife at parting. It was denied him.

In the agony of his soul he rushed from the man who had just bought him, that he might take a farewell of his wife; but his way was obstructed; he was struck over the head with a loaded whip, and was held for a moment; but his agony was too great. When he was let go, he fell a corpse at the feet of his master. His heart was broken. Such scenes are the every-day fruits of American slavery.[1]

There are still separations among husbands and wives. According to clinical psychologist Joseph C. Hammock, Jr., 50 percent of all legal marriages in America end in divorce. Seventy percent of second marriages and 80 percent of third marriages also end in divorce. Frederick Douglass said, "The marriage institution cannot exist among slaves."[2] This is true today. A happy marriage cannot exist among slaves tormented by the master of evil.

But the good master says, "The man who finds a wife finds a good thing; she is a blessing to him from the Lord" (Prov. 18:22 TLB).

Healthy self-image, high self-esteem, and self-worth in a family build a sense of security and confidence among the family members. Christ's purchase sets us free from the fear of parting. We are now able to enjoy the love of God and experience the fulfilled purposes of His perfect will in our lives.

Consider:
Develop a new song of worship for your family.

Pray:
Lord, there are many partings in life, even for Christians, but nothing can separate us from your love which is in Christ Jesus.

CHAPTER 17

A STEADY RHYTHM

See then that you walk circumspectly, not as fools but as wise, redeeming the time, because the days are evil.

Therefore do not be unwise, but understand what the will of the Lord is. And do not be drunk with wine, in which is dissipation; but be filled with the Spirit, speaking to one another in psalms and hymns and spiritual songs, singing and making melody in your heart to the Lord.

(Eph. 5:15–19)

Slaves learned spirituals by repetition.

Work songs, signal songs, and shout songs belong to an oral tradition. Melodies were learned by a steady repetition of words and rhythm. Songs were sung for many purposes and on varied occasions such as baptisms and funerals. "Many a slave's oldest and fondest memory was that of lying on . . . his mother's lap, being 'warmed in her bosom in the cold night of winter,' and hearing her sing . . . him to sleep with a lullaby."[1] Quarter children too young to work in the fields played games to rhythm and song. Songs also signaled secret meetings and the approach of the evil master or overseer.

Handed down from generation to generation slave songs and stories were an essential medium that expressed the experiences and hopes of the quarter community. Slaves secretly sang songs about freedom in their cabins at night. Many rhymes on freedom were originated and sung softly as the slaves worked in the fields. The songs they sang were uniquely their own creations designed to fit the different occasions.

The song, "When We All Meet in Heaven" spoke of togetherness. It is so wonderful to know that our oneness, established on the finished work of Christ at Calvary, is complete. Nothing can separate us from the love of God.

The love of God gives the believer a predictable walk—a constancy in holy living. When we show a steady rhythm of trusting faith in Christ, this is evident and attractive to others. Hopefully, doors of opportunity will open for us to be able to rehearse our unique stories of God's grace. This sharing may help someone learn a new song of freedom.

Consider:
Live out a vital relationship with Christ that will inspire others to join in the singing.

Pray:
Father, help me to have a peppy, catchy, steady rhythm of faithfulness in doing good.

CHAPTER 18

REMEMBER THE SABBATH

Remember the Sabbath day, to keep it holy. Six days you shall labor and do all your work, but the seventh day is the Sabbath of the LORD your God. In it you shall do no work: you, nor your son, nor your daughter, nor your male servant, nor your female servant, nor your cattle, nor your stranger who is within your gates. For in six days the LORD made the heavens and the earth, the sea, and all that is in them, and rested the seventh day. Therefore the LORD blessed the Sabbath day and hallowed it.

(Ex. 20:8–11)

▼

Although America was founded on principles that guaranteed freedom of religion, many slaves were not allowed to attend church. Observing a Sabbath day of rest or holiday was entirely a gift of the master.

Linda Brent, an ex-slave who freed herself at the risk of death, tells how a slave chapel in her community was spitefully demolished:

> In 1821, a slave church was closed when it was discovered that reading was being taught. . . . [A]s late as 1834 there were only five churches in some states built expressly for the use of Negroes. Not a twentieth part of the Negroes attended divine worship on Sundays, there were no Bibles for them, and the Blacks depended for their religion mainly on their own color.[1]

However, there were many European Americans who risked their lives and reputations to aid the slaves. Some Quakers and men like Charles and John Wesley spoke out against slavery. John Wesley believed that "slavery was morally indefensible—to say nothing of its being completely at variance with the Christian gospel."[2]

When slaves attended church, they often recognized great hypocrisy.

[The slave] was confused and outraged by people who would profess to follow . . . Jesus Christ and who would, simultaneously, indulge in such practices as were necessary to maintain the kind of slavery he experienced. He could never understand people who went out of their way to call themselves Christian and fearers of a benevolent and just God, and who at the same time held their brothers in bondage, fomented brutalities, and subordinated everything to money-making.[3]

This sense of religious hypocrisy was particularly upsetting to slaves when clergy was involved. Linda Brent reported that any pastor who had a child out of wedlock was dismissed from his pastorate. Unless the woman was a slave. In that case he was not touched. "When a pastor told the slaves that God saw their disobedience of their earthly masters and, as their heavenly master, he felt offended, the slaves went home highly amused."[4]

Dr. Timothy L. Smith in his writings *Slavery and Theology* said, "the injustices of their bondage; and the attempted teaching of 'grace, mercy, and redemption' by slave owners was not only ironic, but hypocritical."[5] However, as they heard the prayers and the readings from the Bible, some slaves understood the meaning of

God's love for all humanity better than their oppressors.

"Africans who were pressed up against the wall by American slavery's vast assault upon their humanity discovered in the religion of their ... oppressors a faith which helped them reconcile suffering and hope, guilt and forgiveness, tyranny and spiritual freedom, self-hate and divine acceptance. In that faith some of them found the strength to throw off their bonds, and many others the dignity when once emancipated to stand up free."[6]

One such person was Richard Allen. Born 1760, Allen was "one of four children, a slave of Benjamin Chew who was one of Philadelphia's leading lawyers. Endowed from the beginning with great determination, Allen was able to save enough money by the time he was 17 years of age to purchase his freedom. Once free, he dedicated himself with undying devotion to carry on the struggle for the freedom of others. He provided the leadership his people needed in establishing a church of their own. Allen wanted a place of worship where black people would no longer be looked upon as a 'nuisance,' nor exposed to attitudes of indifference, neglect, toleration or oppression. He wanted to prevent black people from 'taking offence at religion itself,' because of the attitudes of the oppressors."[7]

In 1787, Richard Allen, Absolm Jones, and others considered it a duty to build a house (Bethel) where they would be able to worship God under their own vine and fig tree. They established the Free African Society, the first organization by and for African Americans in this country.

The African Methodist Episcopal Church originated from the Free African Society as a protest against the inhuman treatment which the then-helpless people of African descent were forced to accept. Today the A.M.E. Church has a worldwide membership of more than 2.5 million members, and the 1797 motto for the church remains the same today: "God our Father, Christ our Redeemer, man our brother." To Allen, the first bishop of the A.M.E.C., religion was not just theology—it was something to be practiced.

Jesus spoke out vehemently against hypocrisy. He said, "Woe to you, Pharisees, and you religious leaders—hypocrites! You are so careful to polish the outside of the cup, but the inside is foul with extortion and greed. Blind Pharisees! First cleanse the inside of the cup, and the whole cup will be clean" (Matt. 23:25–26 TLB).

The slave acquired the true beliefs of the Christian religion but not the hypocritical practices. Among the slaves there was the

understanding that . . . "There was a great difference between religion and Christianity."[8]
This statement is still true today.

Consider:
Praying for a life free of hypocrisy.

Pray:
Lord, you know me better than I know myself. See if there are any wicked ways in me. Cleanse me and lead me in the way everlasting.

CHAPTER 19

STEAL
AWAY

That at that time you were without Christ,
being aliens from the commonwealth of Israel
and strangers from the covenants of promise,
having no hope and without God in the world.
But now in Christ Jesus you who once were far
off have been brought near by the blood of
Christ.

For He Himself is our peace, who has made
both one, and has broken down the middle wall
of separation, having abolished in His flesh the
enmity, that is, the law of commandments
contained in ordinances, so as to create in

Himself one new man from the two, thus making peace.

(Eph. 2:12–15)

▼

While "official" church meetings were outlawed in many places, more informal prayer meetings were held often. Sincere communication with God strengthened and encouraged the slave to look beyond present, horrid conditions to a brighter, better day.

One slave narrative explained that when the slaves "... go round singing 'Steal Away to Jesus,' that means there going to be a religious meeting that night. The masters before and after freedom didn't like them religious meetings, so us naturally slips off at night, down in the bottoms or somewhere. Sometimes us sing and pray all night."[1]

Slaveowners did not like slaves congregating for any reason. But in spite of that, and even though the fieldworkers came home exhausted at night, slaves would sneak off to the woods for church services and parties. These were opportunities for them to sing and dance away their weariness and pain together and "feel that ecstasy which comes from knowing that one is a human being, not a work animal."[2] Songs like

"Steal Away" and "Go Way Down Yonder" tell the tale of these secret religious meetings.

Men hired by slavers—"paddyrollers" they were called—patrolled the roads and woods around plantations searching out these secret meetings. If a meeting was found, the paddyrollers would break it up and beat whatever slaves they encountered. One paddyroller told a slave, "If I catch you here servin' God, I'll beat you. You ain't got no time to serve God. We bought you to serve us."[3]

Prayer meetings are still a threat to the present-day evil slave master Satan. Men and women, girls and boys, young and old who meet regularly to worship, praise, and petition God are still harassed by the paddyrollers (Satan's demons).

Prayer meetings in most churches today are poorly attended. Even in large congregations only a small percentage of members meet "down in the bottoms" with other believers to praise, worship, and petition God.

The privilege of meeting freely with other believers to pray is a blessing from God. Once we were far from God and without hope. Because of Christ we have been brought close to God. What a joy to have access to the very presence of God through prayer.

One slave said that while a slave he was denied the freedom to pray with others. But even after the signing of the *Emancipation Proclamation,* he was fearful of being harassed when he attended prayer meetings.

The enemy of our soul does not want us to worship God—to come to know him as a loving, personal, caring father. Opposition continues.

Even after we confess Christ as our Lord and Savior, opposition will come in order to keep us from having a close and dynamic relationship with Jesus.

Jesus promises, "For where two or three are gathered together in my name, there am I in the midst of them" (Matt. 18:20 KJV).

The spirituals of my ancestors are true for me today. When we place priority in our good master in prayer, we have more time and energy to accomplish goals. It is good to "steal away" from the rush and hurry-up pace of our daily lives to be in quietness and prayer with Jesus.

Steal away, steal away,
Steal away to Jesus
Steal away, steal away home,
I ain't got long to stay here.

My Lord calls me, He calls me by the thunder;
The trumpet sound within-a my soul,
I ain't got long to stay here.

"Let us not give up meeting together, as some are in the habit of doing, but let us encourage one another" (Heb. 10:25 NIV).

Consider:

Remember that Jesus promised to be with even two or three who meet in his name. Attend a prayer meeting this week. Make a habit of daily, secret prayer.

Pray:

Lord, help me take time this week to bring my praise and cares to you.

CHAPTER 20

UNCLE TOMS

For it is not an enemy who reproaches me;
Then I could bear it.
Nor is it one who hates me who has exalted
    himself against me;
Then I could hide from him.
But it was you, a man my equal,
My companion and my acquaintance.
We took sweet counsel together,
And walked to the house of God in the throng.

                                         (Ps. 55:12–14)

▼

I would like to think that the slaves had unity and a common bond that treachery could not penetrate. But research of narratives of former slaves tells me differently. There were the "Uncle Toms."

Uncle Toms were usually the house servants. They had the most contact with the master and his family and often were even trained for their duties from childhood. Slaves who worked the fields many times hated the house servant because he or she sometimes let plantation owners know the many planned escapes.

One slave said: "They taught us to be against one another and no matter where you would go you would always find one that would tattle and have the . . . master and the overseer . . . pecking on you. They would be trying to make it soft for themselves."[1] There were house slaves, however, who used their positions inside the big house to gain information to help the field hands. In that sense, they did not work "for" the master.

"The few slaves who betrayed their fellow slaves, through jealousy of their scheme or through hope of ingratiating themselves with their masters seem abnormally few, considering the proportionate distribution of such natures in ordinary society."[2]

Jesus had a close band of twelve men who were also his friends. They traveled together for three years throughout the villages, the countryside, and the big city of Jerusalem. They ate, lived, and worked side by side. They witnessed miracle after miracle together. They questioned, grew in knowledge, loved each other and, I am sure, had many happy, enjoyable times together.

But Jesus said of one of his confidants, "'He who shares my bread has lifted up his heel against me.'" After he had said this, Jesus was troubled in spirit and testified, "'I tell you the truth, one of you is going to betray me'" (John 13:18, 21 NIV).

The slave master often rewarded the slave who revealed the plans of escape. Remember, Judas received thirty pieces of silver for his betrayal of Christ.

Today Satan dangles "rewards" in front of those who would betray others. After forty years of marriage, one spouse decides that a younger mate would be better. The younger mate is, seemingly, the reward. But not only does the divorce crush the couple's children and grand-children, but there is a squabble over the family home. The evil master, Satan, betrays.

There are sometimes broken promises among Christians who do not keep their word, but who create heartaches, broken relationships, debts, and lawsuits.

I would like to think that Christians would honor other Christians, but the Scriptures give a clear picture that betrayal of friendships do exist. "It was not an enemy who taunted me—then I could have borne it; I could have hidden and escaped. But it was you, a man like myself, my companion and my friend. What fellowship we had, what wonderful discussions as we walked together to the Temple of the Lord on holy days" (Ps. 55:12–14 TLB).

Consider:
Do not be like Judas, the betrayer, in your heart.

Pray:
Lord God, I want to be like Jesus in my heart.

CHAPTER 21

LOVING FRIENDSHIP

These things I have spoken to you, that My joy may remain in you, and that your joy may be full. This is My commandment, that you love one another as I have loved you. Greater love has no one than this, than to lay down one's life for his friends. You are My friends if you do whatever I command you. No longer do I call you servants, for a servant does not know what his master is doing; but I have called you friends, for all things that I heard from My Father I have made known to you. You did not choose Me, but I chose you and appointed you that you should go and bear fruit, and that your fruit should remain, that whatever you ask the Father in My name He may give you. These things I command you, that you love one another.

(John 15:11–17)

▼

Heaven for the slave would be incomplete without friends. This thought is expressed in many slave songs.

One song entitled "Swing Low, Sweet Chariot" has a verse that says, "If you get there before I do, / Coming for to carry me home, / Tell all my friends I'm coming too, / Coming for to carry me home."

Every advantage was taken by the slaves to be with friends on neighboring plantations. Dances, corn huskings, funerals, and religious meetings were occasions when slaves requested passes from the master to join friends.

We do not have to seek permission to meet with our friend and master, Jesus. We have instant and personal contact with Christ.

Our personal relationship with God through Jesus also helps us build other viable and vital friendships.

Do you need a real friend, one who will be faithful to you no matter what happens? Jesus is that friend. He said, "No longer do I call you servants, for a servant does not know what his master is doing; but I have called you friends" (v. 15). Gladly we claim friendship with the one who loved us so much that he died for us.

Consider:
The last time you practiced the presence of your best friend—Jesus. Block out a day on your calendar specifically for you and Christ to spend in praise, prayer, and Bible study.

Pray:
Dear Jesus, help me tell others that real friendships begin with a personal relationship with you.

CHAPTER 22

A NEW MASTER

And Jesus, when He came out, saw a great multitude and was moved with compassion for them, because they were like sheep not having a shepherd. So He began to teach them many things. When the day was now far spent, His disciples came to Him and said, "This is a deserted place, and already the hour is late. Send them away, that they may go into the surrounding country and villages and buy themselves bread; for they have nothing to eat."

But He answered and said to them, "You give them something to eat."

And they said to Him, "Shall we go and buy two hundred denarii worth of bread and give them something to eat?"

But He said to them, "How many loaves do you have? Go and see."

And when they found out they said, "Five, and two fish."

Then He commanded them to make them all sit down in groups on the green grass. So they sat down in ranks, in hundreds and in fifties. And when He had taken the five loaves and the two fish, He looked up to heaven, blessed and broke the loaves, and gave them to His disciples to set before them; and the two fish He divided among them all. So they all ate and were filled. And they took up twelve baskets full of fragments and of the fish. Now those who had eaten the loaves were about five thousand men.

(Mark 6:34–44)

▼

Slave ships were miserable vessels. The slaves who were too sick to remain in the hold of the ships were kept on the deck. The slave Equiano said,

the stench of the hold was so intolerably loathsome that it was dangerous to remain there for anytime and some of us had been permitted to stay on deck for the fresh air; but now that the whole ships' cargo were confined together it became absolutely pestilential.

. . . I was soon reduced so low here that it was thought necessary to keep me almost always on deck; and from my extreme youth I was not put in fetters. In this situation I expected every hour to share the fate of my companions, some of whom were almost daily brought upon deck at the point of death, which I began to hope would soon put an end to my miseries. Often did I think many of the inhabitants of the deep much more happy than myself. I envied them the freedom they enjoyed, and as often wished I could change my condition for theirs.

One day the slavers caught a large number of fish, . . . and when they had killed and satisfied themselves with as many as they thought fit, to our astonishment who were on the deck, rather than give any of them to us to eat, as we expected, they tossed the remaining fish into the sea again, although we begged and prayed for some as well as we could, but in vain.

Some of my countrymen, being pressed by hunger, took an opportunity, when they thought no one saw them, of trying to get a little privately; but they were discovered, and the attempt procured them some very severe floggings.[1]

It is different under the new master.

One day Jesus and his disciples left in a boat to go "to a quiet place [to] get some rest." The people saw them depart, figured out where they were going, ran on foot, and arrived at the solitary spot before Jesus. When Jesus, who was tired and hungry, saw the crowd, he "had compassion on them, because they were like sheep without a shepherd" (Mark 6:34 NIV). Jesus began teaching them many things.

The day grew late. Jesus and his followers were in a remote place, and there was no food to feed the people. Jesus asked his disciples how much food they had. They counted out five loaves of bread and two fish.

Jesus, "taking the five loaves and the two fish and looking up to heaven . . . gave thanks and broke the loaves. Then he gave them to his disciples to set before the people. He also divided the two fish among them all. They all ate and were satisfied, and the disciples picked up twelve basketfuls of broken pieces of bread and fish. The number of the men who had eaten was five thousand" (Mark 6:41–43 NIV).

The total number of slaves on an average slave ship was approximately seven hundred. Yet the great catch of the slavers was not used to feed even one of the Africans.

Our new Master says all our needs for food, clothing, and shelter will be supplied. "But seek first his kingdom and his righteousness" (Matt. 6:33 NIV).

Consider:
Praise God for caring for our physical needs *and* for giving us the desires of our hearts.

Pray:
Thank you for having mercy and compassion on me.

CHAPTER 23

THE GREAT CHASE

Nevertheless I tell you the truth. It is to your advantage that I go away; for if I do not go away, the Helper will not come to you; but if I depart, I will send Him to you. And when He has come, He will convict the world of sin, and of righteousness, and of judgment: of sin, because they do not believe in Me; of righteousness, because I go to My Father and you see Me no more; of judgment, because the ruler of this world is judged.

I still have many things to say to you, but you cannot bear them now. However, when He, the Spirit of truth, has come, He will guide you into all truth; for He will not speak on His own authority, but whatever He hears He will speak; and He will tell you things to come. He will glorify Me, for He will take of what is Mine and declare it to you.

(John 16:7–14)

▼

When Frederick Douglass gave his famous lectures in England in 1846 on the horrors of slavery, he said, "The bloodhound is regularly trained in the United States, and advertisements are to be found . . . from persons advertising themselves as bloodhound trainers, and offering to hunt down slaves at fifteen dollars a piece, recommending their hounds as the fleetest in the neighborhood, never known to fail."[1]

However, slaves still escaped to freedom even under threat of violence, swamps, snakes, and dogs.

There is a loving, skillfully trained hound of heaven that redeems the sin-slave for his rightful owner. The hound of heaven's purpose is to draw the lost to the Savior. No mere fifteen dollar price tag is placed on the captured. Christ gave his life. He died on Calvary to pay the price of our sin debt in order to return us to our rightful owner.

Still today some people live like fugitives. They are not running for safety . . . they are running from God. And they become separated from God by sin.

I fled Him, down the nights and down the days;
I fled Him, down the arches of the years;
... From those strong feet that followed, followed
  after.
But with unhurrying pace
Deliberate speed, majestic instance,
They beat—and a Voice beat ...[2]

The Holy Spirit, God's hound of heaven, searches high and low for those who have been drawn away from the shelter of the good master. Because when we run away from God, a great chase begins. The Holy Spirit, God's hound of heaven, pursues those separated from God by sin.

Many slaves succeeded in running away from those who were chasing them. But, the Holy Spirit always wins the chase and presents the sinner to his rightful owner—God.

The Christian life is described as a *race* in 1 Corinthians. We are not to run aimlessly but to keep the goal in mind. We will be winners if we exercise self-control and complete the course.

Consider:

Which direction are you running: away from God or toward God?

Pray:

Loving, good Master, I never want to run away from you.

CHAPTER 24

BROKEN POWER

Knowing this, that our old man was crucified with Him, that the body of sin might be done away with, that we should no longer be slaves of sin. For he who has died has been freed from sin. Now if we died with Christ, we believe that we shall also live with Him, knowing that Christ, having been raised from the dead, dies no more. Death no longer has dominion over Him. For the death that He died, He died to sin once for all; but the life that He lives, He lives to God. Likewise you also, reckon yourselves to be dead indeed to sin, but alive to God in Christ Jesus our Lord.

Therefore do not let sin reign in your mortal body, that you should obey it in its lusts. And do not present your members as instruments of unrighteousness to sin, but present yourselves to God as being alive from the dead, and your members as instruments of righteousness to God. For sin shall not have dominion over you, for you are not under law but under grace.

(Rom. 6:6–14)

▼

Chuck Swindoll tells of a man who was laid off a job after fifteen years. The job required a daily fifty-five mile drive to a building with no windows and no fulfillment. "He's free. Freed from a slavery that at times seemed as brutal and demanding as a nineteenth century plantation owner."

Slavery is alive in the twentieth century. Today we have modern versions of slavery: corruption in big business, addictions of all kinds, unlawful relationships, and immoral practices. The result of slavery to sin is broken health, broken hearts, broken finances, broken families, and broken lives.

The good news for this sin-laden world is that the shackles have been broken, the way to freedom from sin is found in Christ. "Consider yourselves also dead to sin and your relation to it broken, but (that you are) alive to God—living in unbroken fellowship with Him—in Christ Jesus" (Rom. 6:11 AMPLIFIED BIBLE).

There are new songs for the whole world to sing when the meaning and purpose for living are realized.

"After all this, there is only one thing to say: Have reverence for God, and obey His commands because this is all that man was created for" (Eccl. 12:13 TEV).

Consider:
You are dead to sin but alive to God.

Pray:
Thank you, God, for breaking the power of sin and death over me.

CHAPTER 25

FREEDOM PAPERS

Blessed be the God and Father of our Lord Jesus Christ, who has blessed us with every spiritual blessing in the heavenly places in Christ, just as He chose us in Him before the foundation of the world, that we should be holy and without blame before Him in love, having predestined us to adoption as sons by Jesus Christ to Himself, according to the good pleasure of His will, to the praise of the glory of His grace, by which He made us accepted in the Beloved.

In Him we have redemption through His blood, the forgiveness of sins, according to the riches of His grace which He made to abound toward us in all wisdom and prudence, having made known to us the mystery of His will, according to His good pleasure which He purposed in Himself, that in the dispensation of the fullness of the times He might gather together in one all things in Christ, both which are in heaven and which are on earth—in Him. In Him also we have obtained an inheritance, being predestined according to the purpose of Him who works all things according to the counsel of His will, that we who first trusted in Christ should be to the praise of His glory.

In Him you also trusted, after you heard the word of truth, the gospel of your salvation; in whom also, having believed, you were sealed with the Holy Spirit of promise, who is the guarantee of our inheritance until the redemption of the purchased possession, to the praise of His glory.

(Eph. 1:3–14)

▼

My dad told me of a time in the early 1950s when blacks needed a picture I.D. (pass) if they were, in his words, "caught walking on the streets after 6:00 P.M. outside the African American neighborhoods." As recent as four decades ago, there were papers that blacks had to carry.

One of the greatest dreams of slaves was to get their *freedom papers*. Yet once the slave received the freedom papers, he could be bought and sold again. The tangible, flimsy freedom papers were easily lost, stolen, or simply ignored. There were no guarantees.

Throughout the slave land, the African was aware of the fight being waged outside . . . of slave holding states to see that he got his freedom. In the eyes of one slave, only his free papers made him a [human being]. This awareness was the basis for this personal struggle to be free, often by risking his life and health again and again.

His songs reveal that freedom to him was more than a thing he personally desired. It was a dream to be fulfilled throughout the life of a man, wherever man lived. It was a song itself. It is remarkable that in the "land of the free and the home of the brave" no literature treats the concepts of freedom with such great respect, endearment, and dedication as the poems created by American slaves.[1]

Another type of papers was the *ownership papers*. Certificates verified that the slave was a piece of merchandise, much like a wagon, a plow, or the animal in the barn.

The movement of all blacks, free or slave, was severely restricted: "In 1842, any free Negro entering the state could be sold out of hand . . . a free Negro with good evidence had trouble withstanding a challenge to this freedom in court."[2] Passes were required for any significant movement in or around the community.

God says to those who believe and trust in his Son that he will give us freedom papers documented in the portals of heaven. Our papers are sealed with an immovable seal: "The Spirit's seal upon us means that God has already purchased us and that he guarantees to bring us to himself" (Eph. 1:14b TLB).

There is no risk of being returned to our old, evil slave masters. There is no threat of losing what God has given. Christ not only gave us freedom papers from sin's slavery, he gave us freedom of body, soul, and spirit.

Consider:
Make sure that your freedom papers are valid with God's seal.

Pray:
Father, thank you that I can trust your Word, and your love for me without fear.

CHAPTER 26

JUBILEE

Then you shall cause the trumpet of the Jubilee to sound on the tenth day of the seventh month; on the Day of Atonement you shall make the trumpet to sound throughout all your land. And you shall consecrate the fiftieth year, and proclaim liberty throughout all the land to all its inhabitants. It shall be a Jubilee for you; and each of you shall return to his possession, and each of you shall return to his family. That fiftieth year shall be a Jubilee to you.

Therefore you shall not oppress one another, but you shall fear your God; for I am the LORD your God.

(Lev. 25:9–11a, 17)

▼

I believe that there must have been someone in my ancestral line who cried out to God for the deliverance of their children's children. Perhaps on a cold night, with no fire or blankets to keep them warm, someone prayed, "Lawd, help us. I don't want my children's children to suffer. We don't need more songs of bondage. We want a new song of freedom."

That prayer was answered because I, along with many others, am free. We heard the gospel and believed that Christ died on the cross for our sins and that he rose from the grave three days later. Because we have received Christ into our lives we have a new slave song. He has done marvelous things for us. Our slavery to sin is abolished! Jubilee!

Have you ever shouted joyfully about salvation? The more we realize the awful, eternal consequences of rejecting God's provision for our salvation the more we will break out in jubilant song. God has done for us what we could never do for ourselves.

I believe some slave long ago must have prayed for my jubilee and yours—our joy in Christ and his completed work on Calvary for us.

Consider:

Plan how you can share the gospel with those you come in contact with who are still enslaved and without a jubilee to celebrate.

Pray:

Lord, I don't want my children or their children to be enslaved to sin. I pray for my seed just as my ancestors prayed for me. Lawd, help us.

CHAPTER 27

CHILDREN OF LIGHT

For God so loved the world that He gave His only begotten Son, that whoever believes in Him should not perish but have everlasting life. For God did not send His Son into the world to condemn the world, but that the world through Him might be saved.

He who believes in Him is not condemned; but he who does not believe is condemned already, because he has not believed in the name of the only begotten Son of God. And this is the condemnation, that the light has come into the world, and men loved darkness rather than light, because their deeds were evil. For everyone practicing evil hates the light and does not come to the light, lest his deeds should be exposed. But he who does the truth comes to the light, that his deeds may be clearly seen, that they have been done in God.

(John 3:16–21)

▼

When Frederick Douglass presented the horrors of American slavery to the British people, he said,

> I expose slavery in this country, because to expose it is to kill it. Slavery is one of those monsters of darkness to whom the light of truth is death. Expose slavery, and it dies. Light is to slavery what the heat of the sun is to the root of a tree; it must die under it.
>
> All the slaveholder asks of me is silence. He does not ask me to go abroad and preach in favor of slavery; he does not ask any one to do that. He would not say that slavery is a good thing, but the best under the circumstances. The slaveholders want total darkness on the subject. They want the hatchway shut down, that the monster may crawl in his den of darkness, human hopes, and happiness destroying the bondman at will, and having no one to reprove or rebuke him.[1]

As a wife, mother, and a descendant of slaves, I want to expose the horror of spiritual slavery.

I want others to experience real freedom from slavery. There are new songs for the entire world to sing. The search for meaning and purpose ends by believing in a person—Jesus.

Jesus said, "For every wrongdoer hates (loathes, detests) the light and will not come out into the light, but shrinks from it, lest his works—his deeds, his activities, his conduct—be exposed and reproved. But he who practices truth—who does what is right—comes out into the light; so that his works may be plainly shown to be what they are, wrought with God—divinely prompted, done with God's help, in dependence upon Him" (John 3:20–21 AMPLIFIED BIBLE).

The slave boats are still arriving. I can hear the galley chains rattling. I hear the screams of those beaten with the whip of the evil slave driver—the slave driver of child abuse, broken marriages, loneliness, oppression, racism, anxiety, phobias, and depression.

In Dr. David Seamands' book *Healing for Damaged Emotions*, the term *slavedriver* is used to describe the emotional illness of perfectionism. The perfectionist is regularly driven to live above realistic possibilities.

Dr. Seamands wrote, "When the slavedriver of perfectionism propels you with that sense of 'ought,' you overstrain your emotional motor, and pay the price for it in chronic depression."[2]

Promiscuity, AIDS, pornography, and adolescent pregnancy are the consequences of poor choices. These are choices the whip of life strikes on each slave's back often impoverishing the futures of the young. Uncontrolled anger that results in violence and pride of all forms also lashes deadly blows of the whip. All blows that beat down joy and blessing are administered by the evil slave driver.

"The person who is willing to pocket his pride, to take a back seat, to play second fiddle without a feeling of being abused or put upon has gone a long way onto new ground with God.

"There is a tremendous emancipation from 'self' in this attitude. One is set free from the shackles of personal pride."[3]

The pitiless, unmerciful slave driver of unforgiveness and depression holds destructive dominion. Dr. Seamands writes of a young woman with hidden hurts and anger that "had emotionally enslaved her to her older sister. What a struggle it was to let go, to forgive what she felt were injustices . . ."[4]

Dr. Ben Carson, the renowned pediatric surgeon said in his book *Gifted Hands,* "My temper will never control me again . . . never again. I'm free."[5]

With prayer and the power of the Holy Spirit they were released and set free from the anger, the pride, and the hateful, competitive states of mind. They were free from the prison and dark control of the evil slave driver, Satan. The light of God's love exposed the darkness in their lives.

Through faith in Christ, we can be emancipated too. Then with Frederick Douglass we will "know that the whip is burned; that the fetters have been turned to some useful and profitable employment; that the chain is no longer for his limbs; that the bloodhound is no longer to be put upon his track; that his master's authority over him is no longer to be enforced by taking his life—and immediately he walks out from the house of bondage and asserts his freedom as a man."[6]

And today we must assert our freedom as people of God. As children of light we should expose others to the light of God's love. "Take no part in the worthless pleasures of evil and darkness, but instead, rebuke and expose them. It would be shameful even to mention here those pleasures of darkness which the ungodly do. But when you expose them, the light shines in upon their sin and shows it up, and when they see how wrong they really are, some of them may even become children of light!" (Eph. 5:11–13 TLB).

Consider:
Expose others to the light of God's sacrificial love.

Pray:
Thank you, Father, that exposure to your light brings life, rather than death.

CHAPTER 28

COME, LET US CELEBRATE

So He spoke this parable to them, saying:
"What man of you, having a hundred sheep, if he loses one of them, does not leave the ninety-nine in the wilderness, and go after the one which is lost until he finds it? And when he has found it, he lays it on his shoulders, rejoicing. And when he comes home, he calls together his friends and neighbors, saying to them, 'Rejoice with me, for I have found my sheep which was lost!' I say to you that likewise there will be more joy in heaven over one sinner who repents than over ninety-nine just persons who need no repentance.

"Or what woman, having ten silver coins, if she loses one coin, does not light a lamp, sweep the house, and search carefully until she finds it? And when she has found it, she calls her friends and neighbors together, saying, 'Rejoice with me, for I have found the piece which I lost!' Likewise, I say to you, there is joy in the presence of the angels of God over one sinner who repents."

(Luke 15:3–10)

▼

Jesus told a parable of a man who lost a sheep and searched diligently until he found it. Then, he invited his neighbors to come and celebrate with him.

Jesus spoke of a woman who lost a valuable coin. She swept the floor carefully and searched in every nook and cranny until she found the coin. Then she, too, called her neighbors and friends together and said, "Rejoice with me, for I have found the piece which I lost!" (Luke 15:9).

I feel as that woman did. I want to throw a party and celebrate! I want to say, "Rejoice with me! I am no longer lost! I am no longer in bondage! I am free. You can be free too."

Emancipation of the soul is more valuable than any lost sheep, lost coin, or precious jewel. Salvation is a priceless gift from God. "For by grace you have been saved through faith, and that not of yourselves; it is the gift of God" (Eph. 2:8).

I have a song of praise. Sing the first stanza with me. "Jesus loves me this I know, for the Bible tells me so."

Consider:
Celebrate by doing something special for someone else.

Pray:
I love you, Jesus. Thank you for giving me a reason to celebrate.

CHAPTER 29

A TOUGH PILL TO SWALLOW

For though I am free from all men, I have made myself a servant to all, that I might win the more; and to the Jews I became as a Jew, that I might win Jews; to those who are under the law, as under the law, that I might win those who are under the law; to those who are without law, as without law (not being without law toward God, but under law toward Christ), that I might win those who are without law; to the weak I became as weak, that I might win the weak. I have become all things to all men, that I might by all means save some. Now this I do for the gospel's sake, that I may be partaker of it with you.

(1 Cor. 9:19–23)

▼

"I's free! I's free!" came the shout across the plantation, across slave row. "I's free. I'm no longer a slave and I will not be treated like a slave," the African American proclaimed.

After the signing of the *Emancipation Proclamation* by Abraham Lincoln, the shackles were broken.

Yet, I am now a servant.

As an African American, servanthood was a tough pill to swallow. All my life I had been taught: Be free. Be servant to no one! Be your own boss. How do you reprogram a mind-set that requires never being a servant? How do you embrace servanthood when your ancestors were slaves?

"And if you want to be right at the top, you must serve like a slave. Your attitude must be like my own, for I, the Messiah, did not come to be served, but to serve, and give my life as a ransom for many," said Jesus (Matt. 20:27–28 TLB).

So being a servant—a slave to the Lord—was difficult for me as a new Christian. However, the Lord, knowing all things, knew my background, my heritage, my thoughts on the degrading term, *servant.* I learned that being a servant and a slave to Christ is to be his friend. Gladly, I claim

Christian servanthood to one who loves me very much. He said, "I no longer call you slaves, for a master doesn't confide in his slaves; now you are my friends" (John 15:15a TLB).

We have an instant and constant relationship with our Lord and Master, Jesus Christ.

Years ago I read this statement and the words made a lasting impression. It is true that possibly "the Holy Spirit will put a strict watch over you, with a jealous love, and will rebuke you for little words and feelings or for wasting your time, which other Christians never feel distressed over. So make up your mind that God is an infinite Sovereign, and has a right to do as he pleases with his own. He may not explain to you a thousand things which puzzle your reason in his dealings with you, but . . . he will wrap you up in a jealous love, and bestow upon you many blessings which come only to those who are in the inner circle.

"Settle it forever, then, that you are to deal directly with the Holy Spirit, and that he is to have the privilege of tying your tongue, or chaining your hand, or closing your eyes, in ways that he does not seem to use with others. Now, when you are so possessed with the living God that you are, in your secret heart, pleased and delighted over this peculiar, personal, private, jealous guardianship and management of the

Holy Spirit over your life, you will have found"[1]
joy unspeakable.

Allow the Lord Jesus to have control of your
life. You will find surrender to his Lordship a
very rewarding experience. It is easy to serve the
one you love.

Consider:

The Lord wants to reprogram your confused
thought patterns and fill your heart with his
love.

Pray:

Lord, with your strength I can fully accept each
claim you make upon my life with joy.

CHAPTER 30

EVERYONE SERVES A MASTER

Stand fast therefore in the liberty by which Christ has made us free, and do not be entangled again with a yoke of bondage.

(Gal. 5:1)

My ancestors did not choose their slave masters. They did not even have a chance to consider if they would remain in their own country. Instead they were kidnapped, chained, put on boats by the tens of thousands, and shipped to a foreign land.

Today we can choose whom we will serve. First, we must realize that God loves us. The Bible says, "For God so loved the world that he gave his one and only Son, that whoever believes in him shall not perish but have eternal life" (John 3:16 NIV). "But God demonstrates his own love for us in this: While we were still sinners, Christ died for us" (Rom. 5:8 NIV).

Second, we must realize that we have sinned and that this has separated us from God. This is what has put us in bondage. Romans 3:23 says, "For all have sinned and fall short of the glory of God" (NIV). Romans 6:23 says, "For the wages of sin is death, but the gift of God is eternal life in Christ Jesus our Lord" (NIV).

Third, God has made a provision for taking away this sin, this spiritual slavery. The provision is Jesus Christ. John 14:6 says, "I am the way and the truth and the life. No one comes to the Father except through me" (NIV). First John 5:11b–12 says, "God has given us eternal life, and this life is in his Son. He who has the Son has life; he who does not have the Son of God does not have life" (NIV).

Finally, we must personally accept Christ into our lives in order to have salvation. Revelation 3:20 says, "Here I am! I stand at the door and knock. If anyone hears my voice and opens the door, I will come in and eat with him, and he with me" (NIV). This is our Emancipation Proclamation.

When we choose Christ, we instantly become His child: "But as many as received him, to them gave he power to become the sons of God" (John 1:12a KJV).

Many slaves were fathered by their owners. They grew up unacknowledged as the children of these men. Even though the child's father was the master and owner of the plantation, the slave child's name was never written in the will as an heir to the property.

It is so different with God as our Father. As children of God, we are also joint heirs with Christ. Our names are written in the Lamb's Book of Life which entitles us to all the treasures of heaven.

All people serve one of two masters. They serve Satan, who brings bondage to sin and death, or they turn to Christ, who provides freedom and life. There is no middle road.

When we respond to Christ, and trust him as our Savior and Lord, we receive freedom from all bondage. Our Emancipation Proclamation is the good news of Jesus Christ's sacrifice for our sins. The alternative to choosing freedom in Christ is eternal slavery—damnation in hell.

My ancestors did not have the opportunity to choose whom they wanted to serve. They were captured by a system that brought much misery into their lives and the lives of their children. But "Don't you realize that you can choose your own master? You can choose sin (with death) or else obedience (with acquittal). The one to whom you offer yourself—he will ... be your master and you will be his slave" (Rom. 6:16 TLB).

Consider:

Whom have you chosen to serve? Serve Christ in all you do today. Read Joshua 24:14–15.

Pray:

I praise you, God, for your love and mercy in providing the way to come to you.

CHAPTER 31

SLAVERY CHAIN DONE BROKE AT LAST

Oh, sing to the LORD a new song!
For He has done marvelous things;
His right hand and His holy arm have gained
Him the victory.
The LORD has made known His salvation;
His righteousness He has revealed in the sight
of the nations.
He has remembered His mercy and His
faithfulness to the house of Israel;
All the ends of the earth have seen the salvation
of our God.

Shout joyfully to the LORD, all the earth;
Break forth in song, rejoice, and sing praises.
Sing to the LORD with the harp,
With the harp and the sound of a psalm,
With trumpets and the sound of a horn;
Shout joyfully before the LORD, the King.

Let the sea roar, and all its fullness,
The world and those who dwell in it;
Let the rivers clap their hands;
Let the hills be joyful together before the LORD,
For He is coming to judge the earth.
With righteousness He shall judge the world,
And the peoples with equity.

(Ps. 98:1–9)

▼

It is recorded that ex-slaves remembered hearing the song "Slavery Chain Done Broke at Last" on April 3, 1865.

"One story had it that imprisoned slaves in Lumpkin's Jail started the song when Negro soldiers marched before their barred windows and that Negroes on the street took it up spontaneously:

> Slavery chain done broke at last!
> Broke at last! Broke at last!
> Slavery chain done broke at last!
> Gonna praise God till I die![1]

In the Old Testament a new song celebrated a new act of divine deliverance or blessing. In the New Testament the theme of the new song is Christ's victorious and redemptive work on the cross. The Bible says, "you were slain, and with your blood you purchased men for God from every tribe and language and people and nation" (Rev. 5:9 NIV).

"Sing to him a new song; play skillfully, and shout for joy" (Ps. 33:3 NIV). In other words, praise him who delivered us. Thank him who gave the blessing of a new song.

Yes, I am the great-great-granddaughter of slaves.

Deep within my heart, I believe that someone on slave row cried out to God for the deliverance of their seed—the generations to come.

Someone cried out, "Lawd, we need a new song. No more songs of woe, darkness, and defeat. No more songs of utter despair, blood, and tears. No more songs of bondage, we need a new song of deliverance."

Often a young slave's desire to be free was awakened by their parents' prayers. Booker T. Washington, educator, advisor to presidents Roosevelt and Taft, and founder of Tuskegee Institute was born a slave. At the age of seven he was "awaken[ed] by his mother kneeling over her children and fervently praying . . . that someday she and her children might be free."[2]

Someone on slave row called out to God for me. To that someone I am forever grateful, and I give humble thanks.

I am that seed. Slavery chain done broke at last.

Consider:

Becoming one of those who unselfishly will pray for the salvation of others.

Pray:

Father, I believe that you answer prayers. I pray that my children and my children's children will know you.

CHAPTER 32

WHOSE SLAVE ARE YOU?

But after long abstinence from food, then Paul stood in the midst of them and said, "Men, you should have listened to me, and not have sailed from Crete and incurred this disaster and loss. And now I urge you to take heart, for there will be no loss of life among you, but only of the ship. For there stood by me this night an angel of the God to whom I belong and whom I serve, saying, 'Do not be afraid, Paul; you must be brought before Caesar; and indeed God has granted you all those who sail with you.' Therefore take heart, men, for I believe God that it will be just as it was told me. However, we must run aground on a certain island."

(Acts 27:21–26)

▼

The apostle Paul claimed that God owned him: "For there stood by me this night an angel of the God to whom I belong and whom I serve, saying, 'Do not be afraid, Paul'" (vv. 23–24).

Whose slave are you?

The good news is that when we receive Christ we have a new owner.

Dr. Billy Graham said, "We have changed masters—just as a slave in the first century might be sold and come under the ownership of a new master, so we have been purchased with the blood of Christ, and we belong now to God."

We decide our future. We make our own choice. Will we be a slave to Christ, or a slave to Satan?

When we belong to God, we experience everlasting freedom. The full purpose of our being, our character, our happiness is dependent on the one to whom we belong.

God is calling us to himself. He is reaching out to us in loving ways. He wants us to be his children. He is asking us to follow him and to be ready and eager to do his will.

Consider:

Plan how you will serve the Lord today as his obedient servant.

Pray:

Dear God, if I have never changed ownership before, I do it now. I want to belong to you. I love you. Save me. Thank you for receiving me.

I ask this in Jesus' name and I sign my freedom papers.

Signed: _____

Date: _____

A WORD FROM
THE AUTHOR

And where the Spirit of the Lord is, there is
liberty.

(2 Cor. 3:17)

▼

Many of my ancestors chose death over chains.
Many rebelled, fought, and committed suicide,
deciding it was better to die trying to be free than
to be worked, starved, or beaten to death by
another human being.

Frederick Douglass told of a slave who was
trying to escape to freedom. He said that

... she was a young woman, barefooted, with
very little clothing on, running as fast as she
could for a bridge.

Three men chased the ... young woman ...
[who was] escaping from the bondage in which

she had been held. She made her way to the bridge, but had not reached it . . . there were two slaveholders on the opposite side of the bridge. As soon as the slaveholders chasing the girl saw them, they cried out, "Stop her!" True to their . . . instincts, they came to the rescue of their brother kidnappers across the bridge. The poor girl now saw that there was no chance for her. It was a trying time.

She knew if she went back, she must be a slave forever—she must be dragged down to the scene of pollution which the slaveholders continually provided for most of the poor, sinking, wretched young women whom they called their property.

She formed her solution; and just as those who were about to take her were going to put their hands upon her, to drag her back, she leaped over the balustrades of the bridge, and down she went to rise no more. She chose death, rather than to go back into the hands of those . . . slaveholders from whom she had escaped.[1]

A slave spoke of death as an escape from the horrors of the slave ship. He said, "I now wished for the last friend, death, to relieve me. . . . [A]lthough, not being used to the water, I naturally feared that element the first time I saw it, yet nevertheless, could I have got over the nettings, I would have jumped over the side, but I could not; and besides, the crew used to watch us very closely who were not chained down to the decks, lest we should leap into the water; and I have seen some of the African prisoners most severely cut for attempting to do so, and hourly whipped for not eating."[2] Harriet Tubman, known as the Black Moses of the underground railroad, said, "Liberty and death. If I could not have one, I would have the other."

Today, people are still looking for a way to escape slavery. A way to be free of the prison bars and the chains of crack cocaine. People want to escape the ropes that tie their hands from profitable employment because they are tied to the addiction of gambling and unpaid debts. People want an underground railroad to a better life. They sometimes try suicide—thinking that they can simply pull a trigger, or jump off a bridge, take a handful of prescription drugs, or slit their wrists in order to gain freedom.

But real freedom goes deeper than physical freedom. Real freedom opens the hidden world of the whole person. Genuine freedom touches the total trichotomy of humanity—body, soul, and spirit. Suicide is not the way to go. Jesus said, "I am the way" (John 14:6a KJV).

Sin plays a cruel mind game. Sin breaks, tears down, and destroys even the strongest slave. It can transform us into bruised, rejected, whimpering, crumbled-up human beings. A *slave*. We are starved for agape love rather than food.

While on a speaking engagement, I learned that a fifteen-year-old had committed suicide a few days before I arrived in the small community. The town was in shock over the senseless death. What happened? Why? This teenager was president of her class, on the student council, a cheerleader—a real go-getter.

The sad note about this story is that this community is Anywhere, U.S.A. In fact, Anywhere, World.

The evil master can cause us to believe that we can escape the hurts, broken hearts, fears, financial stress, failures, disappointments, and spiritual bondage by destroying our physical bodies. This is a false belief.

I think about my life. I had everything: a great marriage, two wonderful, healthy daughters, and a new home. But I was unhappy. Why? I didn't know. I only knew that deep down, real happiness always seemed out of reach. No matter what I possessed it was never enough to satisfy me.

My life seemed to have no purpose. All of the good things that happened to me could not answer the questions that plagued me: Who am I? Why was I born? Where am I going?

Most people would have envied my life. I was raised in a good home, the eldest of four daughters. My mama and daddy loved their children and provided well for us. My daddy, in fact, held two jobs in Miami, where we lived, so that he could send his children to college.

Our parents had concerns about our welfare. I was not allowed to date until I was sixteen-years-old. On the nights that I was permitted to date, I had to be home by 12:00 P.M. And my folks meant *inside* the house by 12 o'clock. I can remember hearing mama making it clear to me that there were to be no phones ringing at 12:00 to say that I was on my way and definitely no sitting outside with my date in the car—but be *inside* the house at 12:00.

I knew that my parents loved me, but I felt I would be happier if they would only give me a little more freedom. I kept these feelings hidden from my family. My unfulfilled search for happiness affected my relations with others. I jealously protected any friendships I developed. I did not want anyone who was my friend to have other friends—this included my mother's or sister's friends.

Then I met Norman Symonette. Friends introduced me to this soldier when he returned to Miami after a two-year duty in Germany. Norman asked me for a date.

He found it hard to believe that a nineteen-year-old college student had to be home by midnight. But Norman and I grew to love each other. When he proposed, I was certain that at last I had found the answers to my questions and real contentment. After a formal engagement party, Norman left for a year of duty in the Vietnam War, and I planned our wedding.

We had a large church ceremony followed by a honeymoon in Jamaica. Then we literally "rode away into the sunset." Our home was in scenic Colorado Springs, Colorado, where Norman was stationed with the Army.

We bought a new home after one year of marriage. Then a daughter, Erika, was born. Three years later another daughter, Stephanie, was born. I had all the good things in life, but I remained secretive with my feelings of dissatisfaction and lack of fulfillment.

One spring, a friend, Delores, invited me to attend a Bible study class, which I refused. I gave Delores some excuse about being too busy, but I thought: What relevance does the Bible have in my life? I am not that bored or unhappy!

Delores was persistent but not a nag. She asked if she could preregister me for the fall session. I agreed—and promptly put it out of my mind. I knew that by fall I would have another line of excuses to give her because I did not feel a need to study the Bible.

That fall my lack of fulfillment and satisfaction was still affecting my life, however. As I had done with the friendships of my youth, I jealously guarded my relationship with Norman. I frequently asked him, "Do you love me?"

"Yes, Lonzie, I love you," he answered.

I did not want to be aggravating so I did not ask often, just two or three times a week or whenever he called home from the office I asked again, "Do you love me?"

Many times he mumbled, "I love you," so his coworkers would not hear him.

Low self-esteem caused me to be a jealous and critical person. Destructive behavior patterns existed. I needed to be needed all the time, and I needed other people or things to make me happy. Because of the evil slave master and his whip called low self-esteem and low self-worth, I was in bondage.

When fall came, I received a phone call that gave me the time and place of the Bible study. I had forgotten all about the preregistration for the class. But I jotted down the information on the calendar. When the day arrived, I determined to attend once in order to keep my promise to Delores, then I planned to drop out of the class.

I did not think that I would learn anything from an old, old book that was written a long time ago about people who lived long, long ago. Besides I was a good girl from a good family. Why would I need to study the Bible? Was I mistaken!

What I learned completely changed my thinking about life.

We were studying the book of Romans. When I first heard that God loved and forgave me, I wondered what I needed to be forgiven for; I was already a good person. I had been raised properly. I had never done anything wrong—certainly nothing more than the average American citizen might do.

But I soon learned that my life fell far short of the perfection required for immortality. With the prospect of discovering more about God's love and forgiveness, I kept attending the class.

I learned that "all have sinned, and come short of the glory of God" (Rom. 3:23 KJV). But I also learned that God showed his love for us "in that, while we were yet sinners, Christ died for us" (Rom 5:8 KJV).

Memory work was a part of the Bible study and I was trying to memorize Romans 10:9: "If thou shalt confess with thy mouth the Lord Jesus, and shalt believe in thine heart that God hath raised him from the dead, thou shalt be saved" (KJV). I took out the words thee, thou and thine that used to confuse me with the King James Version of the Bible and inserted my name.

I repeated this verse over and over, and I suddenly realized that the Scriptures were personal. This verse was telling me that, if

Lonzie confessed Jesus as God's Son and her risen Savior, that Lonzie would find salvation. This old, old book that was written a long time ago about people who lived a long time ago had *my name* in it.

Something beautiful happened that fall morning as I sat alone at my kitchen table. The void that I so long had felt in my life was filled as I received Jesus Christ as my Savior by praying Romans 10:9–10 as my confession of belief in Christ.

Receiving Christ did not solve all my problems, of course, but he provided me with the strength to face them. When blood tests indicated that our daughters had sickle cell anemia, we had a loving Lord to comfort and stand by us. When further tests showed no sign of the disease, we praised him for a miracle.

Job and career changes, loved ones lost suddenly and tragically, a nest emptying of young, sickness, and many other situations have caused me to know that God is faithful to his promise "Never will I leave you; never will I forsake you" (Heb. 13:5b NIV).

As I have studied more and more of God's Word, I have gained a deeper understanding of what life is all about. I finally have the answer for the questions that bothered me so many years: Who am I? What on earth am I doing here?

Where am I going? I now know that I am God's "workmanship, created in Christ Jesus for good works" (Eph. 2:10). I am created by God for his pleasure, presented as a lovely gift to Jesus, and one day I will go and live with him forever in heaven because of my faith in Christ.

Jesus keeps me out of the pit of low self-esteem. I know that God loves me. In turn I can love myself, I can give and accept love. I can now allow others to show me or extend their love to me.

The need to feel worthwhile, the need to belong, the need to be loved and to give love, and the need to feel that there is some purpose to our lives are all basic needs for everyone.

I am *somebody* and so are you. God's estimation of your self-worth and my self-worth is higher than the heavens.

Norman noticed and liked the changes that he saw in my life, and he, too, invited Christ into his life through some other circumstances. Both daughters have become excited Christians, and our family is complete in loving and serving Christ—our escape passage to freedom.

The Son of God comes into your life only at your invitation. His grace cannot be purchased or earned by being a good person or by doing good works. I have found purpose in life. I no longer covet human relationships so much that I stifle them.

Are you looking for purpose, meaning, acceptance, fulfillment, friendships, and happiness that really lasts? Are you looking for freedom from the bondage of low self-esteem and low self-worth? Jesus says, "Here I am" (Rev. 3:20). He is standing at the door of your life right now, knocking, waiting for you to open it for his entrance. It is your choice whether you will open the door of your world, your space, and allow Christ to enter or whether you will allow that door to remain closed. Opening the door of my life to Jesus put within reach what had always been just out of reach—new life; real, lasting happiness that is really called *joy!*

There are many ways to serve the One who loved and gave deliverance from the chains and bars that imprisoned me. One way is by regularly presenting my testimony of vital Christianity— telling others how they, too, can know the escape route to freedom. Once we are set free, we have an obligation to assist those who are still enslaved. The needs of others are ever evident to our eyes. Our ears hear the cries for help from the community. Jesus desires that no one remain in chains. He calls us to freedom by whatever means it takes. He calls—*even by the thunder.*

Your invitation to invite Christ into your life may be a simple prayer. Bow your head and earnestly pray this prayer:

Here and now, Lord Jesus, I accept your passage to freedom. I invite you to enter the very center of my personality. I entrust my life to you. Thank you for forgiving my sin and giving me the power to live a liberated life. From now on I will look to you for direction, love, forgiveness, and understanding. Thank you for giving me new life, fulfillment, and joy.

Strong and Free

They fought to make it to the top
Determined to win,
they never stopped
Striving to be all they could be
Giving up everything,
so we could be free.

Dreaming of freedom and of hope
Trying to relate and trying to cope
Struggling to survive and to escape
The battles of life, and all the hate.

Strong, stable, Black, and smart
My ancestors had strong hearts.
Fighting to win their dignity
My Black ancestors, STRONG and FREE.

Stephanie Symonette

Notes

Preface

1. James H. Cone, *Black Theology and Black Power* (New York: Harper San Francisco, 1969), 37.
2. David G. Myers, *Psychology,* 3rd ed. (New York: Worth Publishers, 1992), 587.
3. Cone, 35.

Introduction

1. Langston Hughes and Milton Meltzer, *A Pictorial History of the Negro in America* (New York: Crown Publishers, 1956), 10.

Chapter 1

1. Roger E. Bowman, *Color Us Christian* (Kansas City: Nazarene, 1975), 74.

Chapter 3

1. Ralph Kendricks and Claudette Levitt, *Afro-American Voices, 1770s–1970s* (New York: Oxford, 1970), 24.

Chapter 4

1. Kendricks and Levitt, 112–113.

Chapter 6

1. John Lovell, Jr., *Black Song: The Forge and the Flame* (New York: MacMillan, 1972), 74.
2. Ibid.

Chapter 7
1. Lovell, 122.
2. Ibid., 195.
3. Ibid., 145.
4. Ibid., 122–123.

Chapter 8
1. Lovell, 5.
2. Ibid., 6.

Chapter 9
1. Ibid., 147.
2. Robert S. McGee, *The Search for Significance* (Houston: Rapha Publishing, 1990), 19.
3. Ibid., 43.

Chapter 10
1. Lovell, 144.
2. William Smith, *Smith's Bible Dictionary* (Grand Rapids: Zondervan, 1978), 595.
3. Cone, 35.

Chapter 11
1. Lovell, 143.
2. Kendricks and Levitt, 40.
3. Hughes and Meltzer, 110.

Chapter 12
1. Lovell, 144.
2. Kendricks and Levitt, 68.
3. William Barclay, *Letters to Galatians and Ephesians* (Edinburgh: Saint Andrew Press, 1972), 10–11.

4. Ibid., 62.

Chapter 13
1. Julius Lester, *To Be a Slave* (New York: Scholastic, 1968), 111–114.
2. Lovell, 121.
3. Ibid., 112.
4. Ibid., 124–125.
5. Kendricks and Levitt, 120.
6. Ibid.
7. Thomas L. Webber, *Deep Like the Rivers* (New York: W.W. Norton, 1978), 218.

Chapter 14
1. Lovell, 124–125.
2. Benjamin Drew, *The Refugee: A North-side View of Slavery* (Reading: Addison-Wesley, 1969), 20.

Chapter 15
1. Lovell, 122.
2. Kendricks and Levitt, 64.

Chapter 16
1. Kendricks and Levitt, 66–67.
2. Ibid., 66.

Chapter 17
1. Webber, 159.

Chapter 18
1. Lovell, 150.
2. Warren Thomas Smith, *John Wesley and Slavery* (Nashville: Abingdon Press, 1986), 91.

3. Lovell, 181.
4. Ibid., 150.
5. Timothy L. Smith, *Slavery and Theology: The Emergence of Black Christian Consciousness in America* in Roger E. Bowman, *Color Us Christian* (Kansas City: Nazarene Publishing House, 1975), 68.
6. Ibid., 70.
7. Richard Allen, Department of C.E. African Methodist Episcopal Church, A.M.E.C. Publishing House, Nashville, Tennessee.
8. Lovell, 150.

Chapter 19
1. Lester, 103.
2. Ibid.
3. Lovell, 116.

Chapter 20
1. Lovell, 93.
2. Fisk Collection, *Unwritten History of Slavery; Autobiographical Account of Negro Ex-Slaves* (Nashville: Social Science Institute, Fisk University, 1945), 9, Webber notes 67–72, 290.

Chapter 22
1. Kendricks and Levitt, 23.

Chapter 23
1. Hughes, 65.
2. Francis Thompson, *The Hound of Heaven* (Wilton: Morehouse-Barlow, 1947), 4, 6–7.

Chapter 25

1. Lovell, 147.
2. Ibid., 158.

Chapter 27

1. Kendricks and Levitt, 72.
2. David A. Seamands, *Healing for Damaged Emotions* (Wheaton: Victor Books, 1981), 123.
3. Phillip Keller, *A Shepherd Looks at Psalm 23* (Harper Paperbacks, 1990), 69.
4. Seamands, 126–127.
5. Ben Carson with Cecil Murphey, *Gifted Hands, The Ben Carson Story* (Grand Rapids: Zondervan, 1990), 59.
6. Kendricks and Levitt, 66.

Chapter 29

1. *Others May . . . You Cannot* (Grand Rapids: Faith, Prayer and Tract League, #76).

Chapter 31

1. Webber, 211.
2. Ibid., 163.

A Word from the Author

1. Kendricks and Levitt, 67–68.
2. Ibid., 21.

Interesting Reading

Cone, James H. *Black Theology and Black Power*. San Francisco: Harper San Francisco, 1989.

———. *A Black Theology of Liberation*. Maryknoll: Orbis Books, 1990.

———. *Christian Classics in Modern English*. Wheaton: Harold Shaw Publishers, 1991.

Douglass, Frederick. *A Narrative of the Life of Frederick Douglass* (1845).

———. *My Bondage and My Freedom* (1855).

———. *The Life and Times of Frederick Douglass* (1892).

Haley, Alex. *Queen: The Story of an American Family*. New York: W. Morrow, 1993.

———. *Roots*. Garden City: Doubleday, 1976.

Hill, Kenneth H., Ph.D. *Drinking from Our Well*. Crown Publishers, 1992.

Johnson, Kenneth L. *Black Theology—Removing the Veil*. Oak Park: Fertile Soil Publishing, 1988.

Perkins, John. *Let Justice Roll Down*. Ventura: Regal Books, 1976.

Symonette, Lonzie. *A New Slave Song*. Colorado Springs: LMS Publishers, 1992.

Wilmore, Gayrand S., and James H. Cone. *Black Theology: A Documentary History*. Maryknoll: Orbis Books, 1992.

About the Author

After moving to Colorado Springs, Colorado, from Miami, Florida, Lonzie served extensively with Stonecroft Ministries, Friendship Bible Coffee Department. She now speaks on vital Christian living to women's groups in Nebraska, Wyoming, New Mexico, and throughout the Colorado Rockies.

Lonzie is completing her education in Biblical Studies and Christian Education. She is an assistant minister at Payne Chapel African Methodist Episcopal Church, a member of the Black Book Writers Network, and owner of LMS Publishers.

She has published many articles in various magazines and newspapers and has written devotionals and Sunday school quarterly lessons. Her first book, *A New Slave Song*, Revised, *He Calls Me by the Thunder,* will be followed by another book, *Everyday Soaring*.